Better Homes and Gardens®

Meredith® Books
Des Moines, Iowa

D1404262

Better Homes and Gardens® 5-Ingredient Grilling
Editor: Jessica Saari
Contributing Project Editor: Linda J. Henry
Contributing Writer: Chuck Smothermon
Assistant Art Director: Todd Emerson Hanson
Contributing Graphic Designer: Diana Van Winkle
Copy Chief: Terri Fredrickson
Publishing Operations Manager: Karen Schirm
Senior Editor, Asset & Information Management: Phillip Morgan
Edit and Design Production Coordinator: Mary Lee Gavin
Editorial Assistant: Cheryl Eckert
Book Production Managers: Pam Kvitne, Marjorie J. Schenkelberg, Rick von Holdt, Mark Weaver
Contributing Photographer: Andy Lyons
Contributing Copy Editor: Michelle Bolton King
Contributing Proofreaders: Sarah Enticknap, Gretchen Kauffman, Susan J. Kling
Contributing Indexer: Elizabeth Parson
Test Kitchen Director: Lynn Blanchard
Test Kitchen Product Supervisor: Marilyn Cornelius
Test Kitchen Home Economists: Elizabeth Burt, R.D., L.D.; Juliana Hale; Laura Harms, R.D.; Maryellyn Krantz; Greg Luna; Jill Moberly; Dianna Nolin; Colleen Weeden; Lori Wilson

Meredith® Books
Executive Director, Editorial: Gregory H. Kayko
Executive Director, Design: Matt Strelecki
Managing Editor: Amy Tincher-Durik
Executive Editor: Jennifer Darling
Senior Editor/Group Manager: Jan Miller
Senior Associate Design Director: Ken Carlson
Associate Marketing Product Manager: Eddie Friend

Publisher and Editor in Chief: James D. Blume
Editorial Director: Linda Raglan Cunningham
Executive Director, New Business Development: Todd M. Davis
Executive Director, Sales: Ken Zagor
Director, Operations: George A. Susral
Director, Production: Douglas M. Johnston
Director, Marketing: Amy Nichols
Business Director: Jim Leonard

Vice President and General Manager: Douglas J. Guendel

Better Homes and Gardens® **Magazine**
Editor in Chief: Gayle Goodson Butler
Deputy Editor, Food and Entertaining: Nancy Hopkins

Meredith Publishing Group
President: Jack Griffin
Senior Vice President: Karla Jeffries

Meredith Corporation
Chairman of the Board: William T. Kerr
President and Chief Executive Officer: Stephen M. Lacy

In Memoriam: E.T. Meredith III (1933–2003)

All of us at Meredith® Books are dedicated to providing you with the information and ideas you need to create delicious foods. We welcome your comments and suggestions. Write to us at: Meredith Books, Cookbook Editorial Department, 1716 Locust St., Des Moines, IA 50309-3023.

Our seal assures you that every recipe in *5-Ingredient Grilling* has been tested in the Better Homes and Gardens® Test Kitchen. This means that each recipe is practical and reliable, and meets our high standards of taste appeal. We guarantee your satisfaction with this book for as long as you own it.

contents

Great grilled food—made easy!

Maxing-out flavor while minimizing ingredients and bother—that's what 5-INGREDIENT GRILLING is all about. The recipes in this book make grilling so speedy and hassle-free, you'll have time to sizzle and sear every day of the week. Treat yourself to whatever type of grilled dish your heart desires—from meat to fish, burgers to poultry. All your traditional favorites taste great when made with 5 ingredients or less.

Even better, there's no need to look elsewhere to round out a spectacular grilled meal. Inside, you'll find 5-ingredient recipes for all sorts of sauces, side dishes, and even desserts. The handy menu section also shows you how to combine convenience items from the supermarket or deli and recipes to whip together multi-course, super suppers in no time. Finally, to top it all off, a bonus chapter of quick serve-along recipes offers inspiring 5-ingredient dishes to prepare in your kitchen that will complete your cookout.

How are ingredients counted in these recipes? Easy. Everything is counted—except salt, black pepper, water, nonstick cooking spray, and any ingredients listed as optional. In other words, what you see is what you get: all the flavor and a fraction of the fuss!

Check out the section of regional menus starting on page 7! Sixteen regional menus have been provided so you can select the perfect supper for any occasion. The four regions of the United States highlighted are the East Coast, Midwest, South, and West Coast. The regions have four different menus, each of which focus on a certain state known for great grilling cuisine. All of the menus use recipes from this book and provide suggestions for easy side dishes you can pick up at the supermarket. When you want to make dinner special, this is the go-to guide for you!

No doubt about it, the 5-ingredient recipes in this book couldn't be easier or more straightforward. But knowing some basic grilling information and terminology will make your results even better and even easier to achieve.

Starting a grill

All grills need some time to heat up to be ready for cooking. Fire up a charcoal grill 20 to 25 minutes before you're ready to grill. A gas grill needs only about 10 minutes of preheating.

You probably don't need any advice on how to start a gas grill—turn a knob, push a button, and you're up and running.

For charcoal grills, consider purchasing a chimney starter. Placed inside your grill, this tall, metal cylinder makes it easy to start coals using newspaper or paraffin starter. Once they're going, you simply pour the burning coals into the grill. Paraffin starter can also be used by itself to start the coals directly on the bottom rack of your grill. But because a chimney starter is vented and holds all the coals above the paraffin, it tends to be more effective than paraffin alone. Lighter fluid is another alternative, but many areas have outlawed its use because of environmental issues.

Whatever you do, invest in a good fire extinguisher and always set up your grill on a non-combustible surface, such as gravel or cement—never on a wooden structure, such as a deck.

Direct and indirect grilling

Direct grilling means cooking food directly over flames or coals. Depending on recipe directions, the grill's lid may or may not be closed.

Direct grilling is perfect for tender, thin, or small foods like burgers, steaks, chops, chicken pieces, and vegetables. Because all of these foods cook quickly—usually in less than 30 minutes—the insides can cook through before the outsides burn from being directly over the flame.

Indirect grilling is best suited to large cuts of meat such as roasts and whole poultry that take a long time to fully cook. To grill indirectly, the food is positioned away from or off to the side of the heat source, and then the grill's lid is closed, making the grill function almost like an oven. This slow cooking technique allows plenty of time for the insides of large foods to cook—without burning the surface of the food over a hot flame.

Indirect grilling setup

To set up a gas grill for indirect cooking, simply turn off the burner over which you'll set the food—the other burner stays on.

For a charcoal grill, once the coals are glowing, push them either to one side or around the outside edges of the bottom grill rack. Place a drip pan—a disposable aluminum pan—underneath the food to catch drippings.

Whichever type of grill you use for indirect grilling, do not repeatedly lift the lid to peek at the food. Each time you lift the lid, valuable heat is lost and it will take much longer for the meat to finish cooking.

Adjusting the heat

Control your grill's heat either by using the control knobs of a gas grill or the top and bottom vents of a charcoal grill. When both top and bottom vents of a charcoal grill are wide open, the grill burns hottest. Partially closing one or both vents reduces the oxygen in the grill, causing the fire to burn cooler.

How do you know whether you're cooking at low, medium, or high temperature? Obviously, if your grill has a built-in thermometer, or if you have an oven-safe thermometer you can set inside (with the lid closed), the task is easy. But what if you don't have a thermometer? Here's a little trick: You can estimate a grill's temperature by holding your hand just above the grill rack (the rack on which the food will be placed) and counting the number of seconds you can comfortably hold it there. Low temperature is 300°F to 325°F or a 6-second hand test; medium-low is 325°F to 350°F or 5 seconds; medium is 350°F to 375F° or 4 seconds; medium-high is 375°F to 400°F or 3 seconds; hot, or high, is 400°F to 450°F or a 2-second hand test.

Meat doneness

The best—and safest—way to know when meat is done is to use an instant-read food thermometer. For big roasts and pieces of poultry, insert the thermometer into the thickest part of the meat, away from any bone or fat. For burgers, steaks, and chops, insert the thermometer horizontally into the middle, away from bone and fat. And, for whole poultry, check the temperature in the thigh—again, away from the bone.

Minimum internal temperature for any ground meat or fresh pork is 160°F, and all poultry should be cooked to at least 170° to 180°F. For beef, lamb, and veal, medium rare is 145°F, medium is 160°F, and well done is 170°F.

The other great thing about using a meat thermometer: Not only are you assured of cooking the meat to a safe temperature, but you're also making it easier to avoid overcooking. After all, unless it's shoe leather you're after, who wants to eat tough, dried-out meat?

Now, on to the menus!

EAST

Moonlight—and Summer Sizzle—in Vermont

Like salt and pepper, Fred and Ginger, Vermont and maple syrup are a perfect pairing. This menu's dishes go together deliciously.

Ready-to-eat baby carrots
with purchased vegetable dip

Maple-Cranberry Game Hens, page 99

Buttered Rosemary New Potatoes, page 193

Goat cheese sprinkled with walnuts
and drizzled with maple syrup

Cranberry juice mixed with sparkling water,
served over ice

New England Seaside Supper

Inspired by the sea and the idyllic New England summer, this simple and creative menu is guaranteed to please.

Purchased spinach and artichoke dip,
served with pita bread wedges

Orange Roughy with Dill, page 113

Mango Mayonnaise, page 181

Easy Roasted Potatoes, page 226

Sliced pineapple, served raw or grilled,
with whole milk yogurt

Pinot Grigio or lemonade

Back East Lobster Party

Everyone knows lobster is a scene-stealer. But with this menu, the supporting cast equally deserves the limelight.

Purchased arugula, sprinkled with fresh fruit and
drizzled with lemon-honey or other purchased
vinaigrette

Lobster Tails with Chive Butter, page 130

Picante Avocados, page 203

Purchased ciabatta or French bread

Purchased shortbread cookies and vanilla ice
cream, drizzled with chocolate sauce

Chardonnay or assorted fruit juices,
served over ice

Big Apple Blow-Out

Just like the big city itself, this flavor-studded menu has something for everyone.

Italian Sausage and Pepper Sandwiches,
page 142

Purchased Greek salad

Purchased potato or vegetable chips

Gorgonzola-Walnut-Stuffed Apples, page 219

Purchased assorted Italian ices

Chianti or favorite sodas

MIDWEST

North Woods Fish Fest

This easy menu featuring your catch of the day will leave you plenty of time to swap stories about the one that got away.

Lemon-Dill Fish Fillets, page 108

Asparagus with Cheese and Chives, page 207

Sliced cucumbers, drizzled with vinegar and oil or your favorite vinaigrette

Blueberry ice cream or lemon sorbet

Sauvignon Blanc or iced green tea, served with orange and lemon wedges

Wisconsin Tailgate Gathering

Kick back before kickoff with good friends, your favorite Wisconsin brew, and these tailgating favorites.

Bratwurst with Kickin' Cranberry Ketchup, page 145

Cheese Straws, page 245

Purchased German-style potato salad

Fruit Wands, page 237

Wisconsin beer or ginger ale

Fresh from the Farm

Hit the farmer's market for a taste of the season's best produce. Then share the bounty with this Iowa-style food fest.

Rhubarb-Glazed Pork Roast, page 45

Farm-Style Green Beans, page 224

Corn on the cob

Watermelon

Iced tea and lemonade, mixed together and served over crushed ice

"Show Me" That Smoky Flavor!

As they say in Missouri, "show me." Here's a menu so delicious your guests will say: "Show me some more!"

Sweet and Smoky Chicken, page 62

Saucepan Baked Beans, page 222

Corn and Tomato Salad, page 205

Purchased peach pie

Root beer

SOUTH

Bayou Boogie Time

All that's missing from this menu are the alligators! But hey, toss an inflatable version in the backyard swimming pool, crank up some zydeco music, and you'll be ready to boogie on the bayou.

Bayou Burgers, page 136

Grilled Sweet Onions, page 201

Purchased pickled okra

Purchased pecan pie

Minted Iced Tea, page 246

South Carolina Barbecue Spread

South Carolina is all about hospitality. You'd better be ready to graciously welcome unexpected guests once these pork chops hit the grill.

Barbecued Pork Chop Sandwiches, page 146

Hot and Sweet Pineapple Slaw, page 234

Purchased boiled peanuts or smoked potato chips

Purchased banana cream pie

Sweetened iced tea

Fire-Kissed Virginia Love Affair

It's said that Virginia is for lovers. This menu proves it's for food lovers as well!

Blackberry-Glazed Ham, page 51

Fire-Roasted Acorn Squash, page 197

Purchased salad greens,
drizzled with raspberry vinaigrette

Purchased peanut pie

Virginia red wine or lemonade

Texas Treat

In keeping with the Lone Star State's best, there's nothing skimpy about this Texas-size meal.

Honey-Bourbon Steaks, page 17

Peppered Steak Fries, page 195

Purchased 3-bean salad or canned black-eyed peas

Purchased hot pickled peppers

Purchased brownies

Texas beer or sweetened iced tea

regional menus

Colorado Cookout

This sublime feast is sure to hit a Rocky Mountain high.

Rocky Mountain Trout, page 116

Summer Green Beans, page 202

Purchased mozzarella salad

Herbed Baguette, page 211

Purchased frozen pound cake,
thawed and sliced, served with
fresh or frozen (thawed before serving)
sliced peaches and whipped cream

Domestic sparkling wine or sparkling grape juice

New Mexico Chuck Wagon

Round up your friends and family for an old-time cookout featuring the hearty goodness of the old Southwest.

Purchased tortilla chips and guacamole

Margarita-Glazed Pork Chops, page 34

Papaya Salsa, page 185 (optional)

Canned pinto beans with green chiles

Shredded iceberg lettuce

Dessert Burritos, page 220

Mexican beer, margaritas, or lime soda

Pacific Pleasures

Overflowing with an abundance of good things from both land and sea, the Pacific Northwest inspires this smorgasbord of signature flavors.

Planked Salmon with
Cucumber-Dill Sauce, page 121

Herb-Grilled Tomatoes, page 200

Purchased coleslaw, garnished with chopped dried
apricots and shelled sunflower seeds

Purchased blueberry pie

Oregon Pinot Noir or apple cider

California Star Party

This showcase of some of California's best and brightest foods tastefully demonstrates why, when it comes to eating, California is a shining star.

Dijon Tuna Steaks, page 112

Chinese Cabbage Slaw, page 233

Purchased fresh fruit salad

Purchased sourdough bread, toasted on the grill

Cinnamon or vanilla ice cream, served with
sliced fresh or dried figs, drizzled with honey and
sprinkled with almonds

California Chardonnay or sparkling water
with freshly squeezed lime

meat

Mustard-Marinated Flank Steak

Slicing flank steak across the grain before serving not only makes for an appealing "fanned" presentation but also makes the beef more tender.

Prep: 20 minutes **Marinate:** 2 to 24 hours **Grill:** 17 minutes **Makes:** 4 to 6 servings

- 1 1¼- to 1½-pound beef flank steak
- ½ teaspoon black pepper
- 1 cup bottled Italian salad dressing
- ½ cup yellow mustard

1. Trim fat from steak. Score steak on both sides by making shallow cuts at 1-inch intervals in a diamond pattern. Rub pepper into both sides of steak. Place steak in a resealable plastic bag set in a shallow dish. For marinade, in a small bowl stir together salad dressing and mustard. Pour over steak; seal bag. Marinate in the refrigerator for 2 to 24 hours, turning bag occasionally.

2. Drain steak, reserving marinade. For a charcoal grill, grill steak on the rack of an uncovered grill directly over medium coals for 17 to 21 minutes for medium (160°F), turning and brushing once with marinade halfway through grilling. (For a gas grill, preheat grill. Reduce heat to medium. Place steak on grill rack over heat. Cover and grill as above.)

3. To serve, thinly slice steak diagonally across the grain.

Per serving: 290 cal., 16 g total fat (4 g sat. fat), 48 mg chol., 730 mg sodium, 4 g carbo., 1 g fiber, 31 g pro.
Daily Values: 1% vit. A, 1% vit. C, 4% calcium, 15% iron

Spicy Ribeyes

Prep: 10 minutes **Chill:** 1 to 2 hours **Grill:** 10 minutes **Makes:** 4 servings

2 12-ounce boneless beef ribeye steaks, cut 1 inch thick
1 tablespoon chili powder
1 tablespoon olive oil
1½ teaspoons dried oregano, crushed
½ teaspoon salt
½ teaspoon ground cumin

1. Trim fat from steaks. Place steaks in a single layer in a shallow dish. For rub, in a small bowl combine the chili powder, oil, oregano, salt, and cumin. Spoon rub evenly over steaks; rub in with your fingers. Cover and chill for 1 to 2 hours.

2. For a charcoal grill, grill steaks on the rack of an uncovered grill directly over medium coals until desired doneness, turning once halfway through grilling. Allow 10 to 12 minutes for medium rare (145°F) or 12 to 15 minutes for medium (160°F). (For a gas grill, preheat grill. Reduce heat to medium. Place steaks on grill rack over heat. Cover and grill as above.)

Per serving: 304 cal., 17 g total fat (6 g sat. fat), 99 mg chol., 402 mg sodium, 2 g carbo., 1 g fiber, 35 g pro.
Daily Values: 12% vit. A, 2% vit. C, 3% calcium, 23% iron

Olive-Stuffed Steaks

Capers, olives, and garlic are each intensely flavored and perfect to partner with one of the richest-tasting cuts of beef: ribeye! See photo on page 81.

Prep: 20 minutes **Grill:** 22 minutes **Makes:** 4 servings

½ cup pimiento-stuffed green olives

3 cloves garlic, minced

1 tablespoon capers, drained

1½ teaspoons finely shredded orange peel

½ teaspoon black pepper

2 boneless beef ribeye steaks, cut 1¼ to 1½ inches thick

1. For stuffing, combine the olives, garlic, capers, orange peel, and pepper in a blender or food processor. Cover and blend or process until mixture is chunky.

2. Cut each steak in half crosswise. Cut a horizontal pocket in each piece of steak, cutting almost to, but not through, the other side. Spoon about 1 tablespoon of the stuffing into each pocket. Spoon remaining stuffing over steaks; rub in with your fingers.

3. For a charcoal grill, arrange medium-hot coals around a drip pan. Test for medium heat above pan. Place steaks on grill rack directly over drip pan. Cover and grill until desired doneness. Allow 22 to 25 minutes for medium rare (145°F) or 25 to 28 minutes for medium (160°F). (For a gas grill, preheat grill. Reduce heat to medium. Adjust for indirect cooking. Place steak on grill rack. Cover and grill as above.)

Per serving: 196 cal., 9 g total fat (3 g sat. fat), 68 mg chol., 375 mg sodium, 2 g carbo., 1 g fiber, 26 g pro.
Daily Values: 2% vit. A, 7% vit. C, 5% calcium, 12% iron

BLT Steaks

See photo on page 81.

Prep: 15 minutes **Grill:** 13 minutes **Makes:** 4 servings

- 2 12-ounce boneless beef top loin steaks, cut 1¼ inches thick
- 8 slices bacon
- ½ cup bottled balsamic vinaigrette salad dressing
- 8 slices red and/or yellow tomato
-    Torn mixed baby salad greens

1. Trim fat from steaks. For a charcoal grill, grill steaks on the rack of an uncovered grill directly over medium coals until desired doneness, turning once halfway through grilling. Allow 13 to 17 minutes for medium rare (145°F) or 17 to 21 minutes for medium (160°F). (For a gas grill, preheat grill. Reduce heat to medium. Place steaks on grill rack over heat. Cover and grill as above.)

2. Meanwhile, in a skillet cook bacon over medium heat until crisp. Remove bacon and drain on paper towels, reserving 1 tablespoon drippings in skillet. Add salad dressing to drippings in skillet. Cook and stir over high heat for 1 minute, scraping up any browned bits. Remove skillet from heat.

3. To serve, halve each steak. Top each steak piece with 2 tomato slices, 2 bacon slices, salad greens, and a splash of the hot dressing from the skillet.

Per serving: 556 cal., 42 g total fat (14 g sat. fat), 122 mg chol., 636 mg sodium, 5 g carbo., 1 g fiber, 38 g pro.
Daily Values: 6% vit. A, 12% vit. C, 2% calcium, 17% iron

Grass-Fed Beef

Rapidly growing in popularity, grass-fed beef is prized by many as a healthy, sustainably grown, and delicious alternative to grain-fed beef.

Because grass-fed cattle feed only on grass or hay, their flavor is often said to be heartier than that of mild grain-fed beef. Grass-fed beef may also be lower in fat while, at the same time, higher in healthful beta-carotene and omega-3 fatty acids. To give it a try, ask around for local sources of high-quality grass-fed beef that is not "finished" on grain.

Top Loins with Gorgonzola Butter

Gorgonzola has a name that sounds like it's from another planet and a delectable flavor that's out of this world. See photo on page 82.

Prep: 15 minutes **Grill:** 10 minutes **Makes:** 8 servings

  2 tablespoons crumbled Gorgonzola or blue cheese
  2 tablespoons tub-style cream cheese spread with onion and garlic
  1 to 2 tablespoons butter, softened
  1 tablespoon chopped pine nuts or walnuts, toasted
  4 boneless beef top loin steaks, cut 1 inch thick
  Salt (optional)

1. For butter, in a bowl combine Gorgonzola cheese, cream cheese spread, butter, and pine nuts; shape into a 1-inch-diameter log. Wrap in plastic wrap. Chill until firm.

2. Trim fat from steaks. For a charcoal grill, grill steaks on the rack of an uncovered grill directly over medium coals until desired doneness, turning once halfway through grilling. Allow 10 to 12 minutes for medium rare (145°F) or 12 to 15 minutes for medium (160°F). (For a gas grill, preheat grill. Reduce heat to medium. Place steaks on grill rack over heat. Cover and grill as above.)

3. To serve, halve each steak. If desired, season each steak piece with salt. Cut butter into 8 slices. Place 1 slice of butter on each steak piece.

Per serving: 268 cal., 19 g total fat (8 g sat. fat), 82 mg chol., 110 mg sodium, 0 g carbo., 0 g fiber, 23 g pro.
Daily Values: 3% vit. A, 2% calcium, 11% iron

Honey-Bourbon Steaks

See photo on page 83.

Prep: 15 minutes **Marinate:** 6 to 8 hours **Grill:** 10 minutes **Makes:** 6 servings

  2½ cups water
  ½ cup bourbon whiskey
  ⅓ cup honey
  3 tablespoons coarse salt
  8 sprigs fresh lemon thyme
  1 teaspoon black pepper
  6 boneless beef top loin steaks, cut 1 inch thick

1. For brine, in a large bowl combine water, ⅓ cup of the bourbon, ¼ cup of the honey, the salt, lemon thyme, and pepper; stir to dissolve salt. Place steaks in a resealable plastic bag set in a shallow dish. Pour brine over steaks; seal bag. Marinate in the refrigerator for 6 to 8 hours, turning bag occasionally. In a small bowl combine the remaining bourbon and the remaining honey; cover and chill.

2. Drain steaks, discarding brine. Rinse steaks and pat dry with paper towels. Remove reserved bourbon mixture from refrigerator.

3. For a charcoal grill, grill steaks on the rack of an uncovered grill directly over medium coals until desired doneness, turning once halfway through grilling. Allow 10 to 12 minutes for medium rare (145°F) or 12 to 15 minutes for medium (160°F). (For a gas grill, preheat grill. Reduce heat to medium. Place steaks on grill rack over heat. Cover and grill as above.)

4. To serve, drizzle steaks with the reserved bourbon mixture. If desired, serve with *watermelon* and *cherry tomatoes.*

Per serving: 375 cal., 12 g total fat (4 g sat. fat), 133 mg chol., 436 mg sodium, 8 g carbo., 0 g fiber, 49 g pro.
Daily Values: 1% calcium, 22% iron

Flat-Iron Steaks

A quick and easy dry rub makes flat-iron steaks flat-out tasty in no time . . . flat. See photo on page 83.

Prep: 10 minutes **Chill:** 2 to 24 hours **Grill:** 7 minutes **Makes:** 6 servings

  1 tablespoon dried marjoram, crushed
  ½ teaspoon garlic salt
  ½ teaspoon black pepper
  4 beef shoulder top blade (flat-iron) steaks, cut ¾ inch thick

1. For rub, in a small bowl combine marjoram, garlic salt, and pepper. Sprinkle rub evenly over both sides of steaks; rub in with your fingers. If desired, cover and chill for 2 to 24 hours.

2. For a charcoal grill, grill steaks on the rack of an uncovered grill directly over medium coals until desired doneness, turning once halfway through grilling. Allow 7 to 9 minutes for medium rare (145°F) or 10 to 12 minutes for medium (160°F). (For a gas grill, preheat grill. Reduce heat to medium. Place steaks on grill rack over heat. Cover and grill as above.)

Per serving: 132 cal., 5 g total fat (2 g sat. fat), 53 mg chol., 129 mg sodium, 1 g carbo., 0 g fiber, 20 g pro.
Daily Values: 1% calcium, 17% iron

Flat-Iron Steaks

Who'd-a thunk it? That a cut from the chuck—usually considered a less tender section of beef—would be one of the most tender cuts around? Better still, flat-iron steaks contain plenty of flavorful marbling and are often cheaper than more popular steaks such as ribeye and T-bone! If you don't see steaks labeled "flat-iron" in your butcher's case, don't panic. They may also be marketed as "beef shoulder top blade steaks."

Peppered T-Bones with Horseradish Mayo

Prep: 20 minutes **Grill:** 18 minutes **Makes:** 4 to 6 servings

- ½ cup mayonnaise or salad dressing
- 2 tablespoons vinegar
- 1 to 2 tablespoons prepared horseradish
- 1 tablespoon snipped fresh parsley (optional)
- 4 beef T-bone or porterhouse steaks, cut 1½ inches thick
- 1 teaspoon cracked black pepper

1. In a small bowl combine mayonnaise, vinegar, horseradish, and, if desired, parsley. Set mayonnaise mixture aside.

2. Trim fat from steaks. Rub pepper into both sides of steaks with your fingers.

3. For a charcoal grill, grill steaks on the rack of an uncovered grill directly over medium coals until desired doneness, turning once halfway through grilling. Allow 18 to 21 minutes for medium rare (145°F) or 22 to 25 minutes for medium (160°F). (For a gas grill, preheat grill. Reduce heat to medium. Place steaks on grill rack over heat. Cover and grill as above.) Serve steaks with mayonnaise mixture.

Per serving: 638 cal., 40 g total fat (9 g sat. fat), 167 mg chol., 335 mg sodium, 1 g carbo., 0 g fiber, 65 g pro.
Daily Values: 2% vit. C, 2% calcium, 61% iron

Zesty Grilled Sirloin

Cooking with dried chile peppers can be surprisingly easy. A short soak, plus a whir in the blender, unlocks their mysteriously complex flavor.

Prep: 20 minutes **Soak:** 30 minutes **Marinate:** 24 hours
Grill: 20 minutes **Makes:** 12 servings

   7 or 8 dried ancho or pasilla chile peppers (about 1½ ounces)
   1 tablespoon ground cumin
   ½ cup olive oil
   2¾ to 3 pounds boneless beef sirloin steak, cut 2 inches thick

1. Wearing plastic or rubber gloves, use scissors or a sharp knife to remove the stalk end from the peppers. Split peppers; remove and discard seeds. In a skillet toast peppers (without oil) over medium heat for 3 to 4 minutes or until they give off a fragrance, turning once or twice with tongs.

2. Transfer peppers to a small bowl. Cover with hot water; soak for 30 minutes. Drain peppers, reserving 1 cup of the soaking water. Place peppers in a blender or food processor.

3. In the same skillet, toast the cumin over medium heat for 1 to 2 minutes or until fragrant, stirring often. Place cumin and olive oil in blender or food processor with peppers. Blend or process until nearly smooth, adding enough of the soaking water to make a medium-thick paste. Set aside.

4. Trim fat from steak. Place steak in a resealable plastic bag set in a shallow dish. Spread pepper paste over both sides of steak; close bag. Marinate in refrigerator for 24 hours, turning bag occasionally.

5. Drain steak, reserving marinade. For a charcoal grill, grill steak on the rack of an uncovered grill directly over medium coals to desired doneness, turning once halfway through grilling and brushing occasionally with reserved marinade during the first half of grilling. Allow 20 to 24 minutes for medium rare (145°F) and 24 to 28 minutes for medium (160°F). (For a gas grill, preheat grill. Reduce heat to medium. Place steak on grill rack over heat. Cover and grill as above.) Discard remaining marinade.

6. To serve, thinly slice steak across the grain.

Per serving: 186 cal., 9 g total fat (2 g sat. fat), 63 mg chol., 56 mg sodium, 3 g carbo., 1 g fiber, 23 g pro.
Daily Values: 19% vit. A, 2% vit. C, 1% calcium, 16% iron

Sirloin with Sour Cream-Mustard Sauce

Prep: 10 minutes **Grill:** 14 minutes **Makes:** 4 servings

- 1½ pounds boneless beef sirloin steak, cut 1 inch thick
- 2 teaspoons garlic-pepper seasoning
- ½ cup dairy sour cream
- 2 tablespoons Dijon-style mustard
- 1 tablespoon snipped fresh chives

1. Trim fat from steak. Rub 1½ teaspoons of the garlic-pepper seasoning onto both sides of steak with your fingers. For a charcoal grill, grill steak on the rack of an uncovered grill directly over medium coals until desired doneness, turning once halfway through grilling. Allow 14 to 18 minutes for medium rare (145°F) and 18 to 22 minutes for medium (160°F). (For a gas grill, preheat grill. Reduce heat to medium. Place steak on grill rack over heat. Cover and grill as above.)

2. Meanwhile, for sauce, in a small bowl combine the remaining ½ teaspoon garlic-pepper seasoning, the sour cream, mustard, and chives.

3. To serve, spoon sauce over steak.

Per serving: 277 cal., 12 g total fat (5 g sat. fat), 114 mg chol., 619 mg sodium, 2 g carbo., 0 g fiber, 37 g pro.
Daily Values: 5% vit. A, 1% vit. C, 5% calcium, 25% iron

Beef Kabobs with Blue Cheese Dipping Sauce

Prep: 20 minutes **Grill:** 8 minutes **Makes:** 4 servings

  1 pound boneless beef sirloin steak, cut 1 inch thick

  2 teaspoons steak seasoning

12 fresh cremini mushrooms, halved

  6 green onions, cut into 2-inch pieces

  1 cup bottled blue cheese salad dressing

1. Trim fat from steak. Cut steak into 1-inch cubes. In a medium bowl combine steak cubes and steak seasoning; toss to coat. On eight 8-inch metal skewers, alternately thread steak cubes, mushrooms, and green onions, leaving a ¼-inch space between pieces.

2. For a charcoal grill, grill kabobs on the rack of an uncovered grill directly over medium coals for 8 to 12 minutes for medium (160°F), turning once halfway through grilling. (For a gas grill, preheat grill. Reduce heat to medium. Place kabobs on grill rack over heat. Cover and grill as above.)

3. Serve kabobs with salad dressing.

Per serving: 475 cal., 38 g total fat (8 g sat. fat), 79 mg chol., 1,071 mg sodium, 8 g carbo., 1 g fiber, 29 g pro.
Daily Values: 8% vit. A, 9% vit. C, 8% calcium, 20% iron

Deviled Steaks

Taking just seconds to whip together, a spirited brush-on sauce makes Deviled Steaks diabolically simple and sinfully delicious.

Prep: 5 minutes **Grill:** 10 minutes **Makes:** 4 servings

- 1 tablespoon ketchup
- 1 tablespoon water
- 1 tablespoon Worcestershire sauce
- 1 teaspoon dry mustard
- ¼ teaspoon salt
- Dash black pepper
- 4 beef tenderloin steaks, cut 1 inch thick

1. For sauce, combine ketchup, water, Worcestershire sauce, mustard, salt, and pepper. Set sauce aside.

2. Trim fat from steaks. For a charcoal grill, grill steaks on the rack of an uncovered grill directly over medium coals until desired doneness, turning once and brushing with some of the sauce halfway through grilling. Allow 10 to 12 minutes for medium rare (145°F) or 12 to 15 minutes for medium (160°F). (For a gas grill, preheat grill. Place steaks on grill rack over heat. Cover and grill as above.)

3. Brush steaks with any remaining sauce before serving.

Per serving: 186 cal., 9 g total fat (3 g sat. fat), 70 mg chol., 288 mg sodium, 2 g carbo., 0 g fiber, 24 g pro.
Daily Values: 1% vit. A, 1% vit. C, 1% calcium, 18% iron

Five-Spice Tri-Tip Roast

Prep: 10 minutes **Chill:** 2 to 4 hours **Grill:** 35 minutes **Stand:** 15 minutes **Makes:** 6 servings

  1 1½- to 2-pound boneless beef tri-tip roast (bottom sirloin)
  1 tablespoon toasted sesame oil
  2 teaspoons five-spice powder
  ½ teaspoon salt

1. Trim fat from roast. In a small bowl combine sesame oil, five-spice powder, and salt. Rub oil mixture evenly over roast with your fingers. Place roast in a resealable plastic bag; seal bag. Refrigerate for 2 to 4 hours.

2. For a charcoal grill, arrange medium-hot coals around a drip pan. Test for medium heat above the pan. Place roast on grill rack over drip pan. Cover and grill until desired doneness. Allow 35 to 40 minutes for medium rare (135°F) and 40 to 45 minutes for medium (150°F). (For a gas grill, preheat grill. Reduce heat to medium. Adjust grill for indirect cooking. Grill as above.)

3. Remove roast from grill. Cover with foil and let stand for 15 minutes before slicing. (The meat's temperature will rise 10°F during standing.)

Per serving: 211 cal., 12 g total fat (4 g sat. fat), 74 mg chol., 253 mg sodium, 1 g carbo., 0 g fiber, 24 g pro.
Daily Values: 4% calcium, 11% iron

Tri-Tip Tip-Off

Long kept secret by West Coast grillers in the know, beef tri-tip roasts are now gaining popularity with pitmasters from sea to shining sea. This naturally tender, triangular-shape cut comes from the bottom sirloin, a section of beef known for hearty flavor. It can be grilled as a whole roast or cut into steaks. Either way, tri-tip is tender enough that it doesn't require marinating and can be grilled either direct or "low and slow" with indirect heat.

Herbed Rib Roast

Get ready for the accolades of a captivated audience as you carve into this herb-encrusted rib roast, a grilling tour de force.

Prep: 10 minutes **Grill:** 2 hours **Stand:** 15 minutes **Makes:** 10 to 12 servings

  1 6-pound beef rib roast
  2 tablespoons finely chopped onion
  4 teaspoons black pepper
  1 teaspoon dried basil, crushed
  1 teaspoon dried thyme, crushed
  ¾ teaspoon salt
  1 tablespoon olive oil or cooking oil

1. Trim fat from roast. For rub, combine onion, pepper, basil, thyme, and salt. Brush roast with oil. Sprinkle rub evenly over roast; rub in with your fingers. Insert a meat thermometer into center of roast without touching bone.

2. For a charcoal grill, arrange medium coals around a drip pan. Test for medium-low heat above pan. Place roast, bone side down, on grill rack over drip pan. Cover and grill until meat thermometer registers desired doneness. Allow 2 to 2¾ hours for medium rare (135°F) or 2½ to 3¼ hours for medium (150°F). (For a gas grill, preheat grill. Reduce heat to medium-low. Adjust for indirect cooking. Grill as above.)

3. Remove roast from grill. Cover with foil and let stand for 15 minutes before slicing. (The meat's temperature will rise 10°F during standing.)

Per serving: 258 cal., 12 g total fat (4 g sat. fat), 95 mg chol., 262 mg sodium, 1 g carbo., 0 g fiber, 33 g pro.
Daily Values: 1% vit. A, 1% vit. C, 2% calcium, 22% iron

Chili-Rubbed Prime Rib

See photo on page *84*.

Prep: 20 minutes **Grill:** 2 hours **Stand:** 15 minutes **Makes:** 10 to 12 servings

    1 4- to 5-pound beef rib roast
    2 tablespoons hot Mexican-style chili powder or chili powder
    1 tablespoon unsweetened cocoa powder
    ½ teaspoon coarse salt
    ½ teaspoon black pepper
    1 tablespoon olive oil
    1 recipe Citrus Butter (page 187) (optional)

1. Trim fat from roast. For rub, in a small bowl combine chili powder, cocoa powder, salt, and pepper. Brush roast with oil. Sprinkle rub evenly over roast; rub in with your fingers.

2. For a charcoal grill, arrange medium coals around a drip pan. Test for medium-low heat above pan. Place roast, bone side down, on grill rack over drip pan. Cover and grill to desired doneness. Allow 2 to 2¾ hours for medium rare (135°F) or 2½ to 3¼ hours for medium (150°F). (For a gas grill, preheat grill. Reduce heat to medium-low. Adjust for indirect cooking. Place roast, bone side down, on grill rack. Grill as above.)

3. Remove roast from grill. Cover with foil and let stand 15 minutes before slicing. (The meat's temperature will rise 10°F during standing.) If desired, serve with Citrus Butter.

Per serving: 226 cal., 15 g total fat (6 g sat. fat), 61 mg chol., 168 mg sodium, 1 g carbo., 1 g fiber, 21 g pro.
Daily Values: 9% vit. A, 2% vit. C, 2% calcium, 14% iron

Veal Chops with Ginger Butter

Creamy butter scented with ginger, shallot, and tarragon creates its own luxurious sauce as it melts into fork-tender veal.

Prep: 15 minutes **Grill:** 12 minutes **Makes:** 4 servings

- ¼ cup butter, softened
- 2 tablespoons chopped crystallized ginger
- 1 tablespoon chopped shallot
- 1 tablespoon snipped fresh tarragon
- 4 veal loin chops, cut about 1 inch thick
- Salt and black pepper

1. In a small bowl combine butter, ginger, shallot, and tarragon; set butter mixture aside.

2. Trim fat from chops; sprinkle with salt and pepper. For a charcoal grill, grill chops on the rack of an uncovered grill directly over medium coals for 12 to 15 minutes for medium (160°F), turning once halfway through grilling. (For a gas grill, preheat grill. Reduce heat to medium. Place chops on grill rack over heat. Cover and grill as above.)

3. To serve, top each chop with 1 tablespoon of the butter mixture.

Per serving: 251 cal., 16 g total fat (9 g sat. fat), 123 mg chol., 358 mg sodium, 3 g carbo., 0 g fiber, 23 g pro.
Daily Values: 10% vit. A, 2% calcium, 5% iron

Veal Chops with Apples

Prep: 10 minutes **Marinate:** 6 to 24 hours **Grill:** 10 minutes **Makes:** 4 servings

    4 boneless veal top loin chops, cut ¾ inch thick
    ½ cup dry white wine
    2 tablespoons cooking oil
    2 teaspoons dried sage, crushed
    ½ teaspoon salt
    ½ teaspoon black pepper
    2 medium tart cooking apples

1. Trim fat from chops. Place chops in a resealable plastic bag set in a shallow dish. For marinade, in a small bowl combine wine, oil, sage, salt, and pepper. Pour over chops; seal bag. Marinate in the refrigerator for 6 to 24 hours, turning bag occasionally.

2. Drain chops, reserving marinade. Just before grilling, core apples; cut crosswise into 1-inch slices.

3. For a charcoal grill, grill chops and apple slices on the rack of an uncovered grill directly over medium coals for 10 to 12 minutes for medium (160°F), turning and brushing once with marinade halfway through grilling. (For a gas grill, preheat grill. Reduce heat to medium. Place chops and apple slices on grill rack over heat. Cover and grill as above.)

4. Serve chops with apple slices.

Per serving: 271 cal., 13 g total fat (3 g sat. fat), 95 mg chol., 354 mg sodium, 9 g carbo., 1 g fiber, 24 g pro.
Daily Values: 5% vit. C, 2% calcium, 7% iron

Veal Rolls Stuffed with Herb Cheese

If you don't have a meat mallet, grab a small skillet or saucepan to pound the veal. Either works just fine. See photo on page 84.

Prep: 25 minutes **Grill:** 20 minutes **Makes:** 4 servings

    1 pound boneless veal round steak

    4 ounces haricots verts or tiny young green beans

    4 tablespoons semisoft cheese with garlic and herb

    4 slices prosciutto (about 2½ ounces)

    2 tablespoons butter or margarine, melted

1. Trim fat from meat. Cut into 4 serving-size pieces. Place meat between 2 pieces of plastic wrap. Working from center to edges, use the flat side of a meat mallet to pound meat to ¼-inch thickness. Remove plastic wrap.

2. Trim beans; cook, covered, in lightly salted boiling water for 4 minutes. Drain.

3. Spread each veal piece with cheese. Top with one-fourth of the beans and a slice of prosciutto (trim beans and fold prosciutto if necessary to fit). Fold in sides; roll up meat. Seal edges with wooden toothpicks or small metal skewers. Brush rolls with melted butter.

4. For a charcoal grill, arrange medium-hot coals around a drip pan. Test for medium heat above the pan. Place meat rolls on grill rack over drip pan. Cover and grill for 20 to 24 minutes for medium (160°F), turning once halfway through grilling. (For a gas grill, preheat grill. Reduce heat to medium. Adjust for indirect cooking. Grill as above.)

5. To serve, remove toothpicks or skewers from meat rolls.

Per serving: 245 cal., 12 g total fat (7 g sat. fat), 117 mg chol., 641 mg sodium, 2 g carbo., 1 g fiber, 30 g pro.
Daily Values: 8% vit. A, 6% vit. C, 2% calcium, 7% iron

Lamb Chops with Mint Marinade

The combination of tender grilled lamb and refreshing mint has passed the test of time.

Prep: 10 minutes **Marinate:** 30 minutes to 24 hours **Grill:** 12 minutes **Makes:** 4 servings

     8 lamb loin chops, cut 1 inch thick
     2 tablespoons lemon juice
     2 tablespoons olive oil
     ¼ cup snipped fresh mint
  1½ teaspoons bottled minced garlic
     ¼ teaspoon black pepper
     ¼ teaspoon salt

1. Trim fat from chops. Place chops in a resealable plastic bag set in a shallow dish. For marinade, combine lemon juice, oil, 3 tablespoons of the mint, the garlic, and pepper. Pour marinade over chops; seal bag. Marinate in the refrigerator for at least 30 minutes or up to 24 hours, turning bag occasionally.

2. Drain chops, discarding marinade. Sprinkle chops with salt. For charcoal grill, grill chops on rack of an uncovered grill directly over medium coals until desired doneness, turning once halfway through grilling. Allow 12 to 14 minutes for medium rare (145°F) or 15 to 17 minutes for medium (160°F). (For a gas grill, preheat grill. Reduce heat to medium. Place chops on grill rack over heat. Cover and grill as above.)

3. To serve, sprinkle chops with the remaining mint.

Per serving: 236 cal., 13 g total fat (3 g sat. fat), 80 mg chol., 217 mg sodium, 2 g carbo., 0 g fiber, 26 g pro.
Daily Values: 13% vit. C, 3% calcium, 18% iron

Herbed Lamb Chops

Prep: 15 minutes **Marinate:** 4 to 24 hours **Grill:** 12 minutes **Makes:** 4 servings

    8 lamb rib chops, cut 1 inch thick
    ½ cup dry white wine
    2 tablespoons snipped fresh oregano, basil, and/or thyme
    2 tablespoons olive oil
    ½ teaspoon salt
    ¼ teaspoon black pepper
    2 cloves garlic, minced

1. Place chops in a resealable plastic bag set in a shallow dish. For marinade, in a small bowl combine wine, desired herb, oil, salt, pepper, and garlic. Pour over chops; seal bag. Marinate in the refrigerator for 4 to 24 hours, turning bag occasionally.

2. Drain chops, discarding marinade. For a charcoal grill, grill chops on the rack of an uncovered grill directly over medium coals until desired doneness, turning once halfway through grilling. Allow 12 to 14 minutes for medium rare (145°F) or 15 to 17 minutes for medium (160°F). (For a gas grill, preheat grill. Reduce heat to medium. Place chops on grill rack over heat. Cover and grill as above.)

Per serving: 309 cal., 17 g total fat (6 g sat. fat), 112 mg chol., 195 mg sodium, 0 g carbo., 0 g fiber, 34 g pro.
Daily Values: 1% vit. C, 2% calcium, 16% iron

Lemon-Pepper Lamb

Prep: 10 minutes **Grill:** 1½ hours **Stand:** 15 minutes **Makes:** 8 servings

1 2- to 3-pound boneless rolled lamb shoulder roast
1 teaspoon lemon-pepper seasoning
1 teaspoon dried marjoram, crushed
2 cloves garlic, minced

1. Trim fat from roast. For rub, in a small bowl combine lemon-pepper seasoning, marjoram, and garlic. Sprinkle rub evenly over roast; rub in with your fingers.

2. For a charcoal grill, arrange medium coals around a drip pan. Test for medium-low heat above the pan. Place roast on grill rack over drip pan. Cover and grill until desired doneness. Allow 1½ to 2 hours for medium rare (135°F) or 2¼ to 2½ hours for medium (150°F). (For a gas grill, preheat grill. Reduce heat to medium-low. Adjust for indirect cooking. Grill as above.)

3. Remove roast from grill. Cover with foil and let stand for 15 minutes before slicing. (The meat's temperature will rise 10°F during standing.)

Per serving: 148 cal., 6 g total fat (2 g sat. fat), 72 mg chol., 195 mg sodium, 0 g carbo., 0 g fiber, 23 g pro.
Daily Values: 2% calcium, 13% iron

Polish Sausage Foil Dinner

Prep: 5 minutes **Grill:** 15 minutes **Stand:** 5 minutes **Makes:** 4 servings

  4 cups frozen loose-pack diced hash brown potatoes with onions and peppers, thawed

12 ounces cooked smoked sausage, sliced

¼ cup bottled Italian salad dressing

¼ cup shredded cheddar cheese

1. Tear off a 24×12-inch piece of heavy foil; fold in half to make a 12-inch square. Place potatoes and sausage in center of foil square. Drizzle salad dressing over potatoes and sausage. Bring up two opposite edges of foil and seal with a double fold. Fold remaining edges together to completely enclose the mixture, leaving space for steam to build.

2. For a charcoal grill, grill foil packet on the rack of an uncovered grill directly over medium coals about 15 minutes or until potatoes are tender, turning packet over once halfway through grilling. (For a gas grill, preheat grill. Reduce heat to medium. Place foil packet on grill rack over heat. Cover and grill as above.)

3. Remove foil packet from grill; open carefully. Sprinkle with cheese. Reseal foil packet; let stand about 5 minutes or until cheese melts.

Per serving: 474 cal., 34 g total fat (12 g sat. fat), 66 mg chol., 1,581 mg sodium, 18 g carbo., 2 g fiber, 22 g pro.
Daily Values: 2% vit. A, 14% vit. C, 9% calcium, 8% iron

Margarita-Glazed Pork Chops

These tart, citrus-glazed chops get a kick from jalapeño and ginger. For even more tang, substitute lime juice for the tequila.

Prep: 10 minutes **Grill:** 7 minutes **Makes:** 4 servings

    4 boneless pork loin chops, cut 1 inch thick
    ⅓ cup orange marmalade
    2 tablespoons tequila or lime juice
    1 fresh jalapeño chile pepper, seeded and finely chopped (see tip, below)
    1 teaspoon grated fresh ginger or ½ teaspoon ground ginger

1. Trim fat from chops. For glaze, in a small bowl combine orange marmalade, tequila, chile pepper, and ginger. Set glaze aside.

2. For a charcoal grill, grill chops on the rack of an uncovered grill directly over medium coals for 7 to 9 minutes or until chops are slightly pink in center and juices run clear (160°F), turning once halfway through grilling and brushing frequently with glaze during the last 10 minutes of grilling. (For a gas grill, preheat grill. Reduce heat to medium. Place chops on grill rack over heat. Cover and grill as above.)

Per serving: 314 cal., 8 g total fat (3 g sat. fat), 106 mg chol., 117 mg sodium, 18 g carbo., 0 g fiber, 38 g pro.
Daily Values: 2% vit. A, 8% vit. C, 4% calcium, 7% iron

Working with Hot Chile Peppers

Hot chiles contain volatile oils that will burn not only your tongue but your skin and eyes too if you're not careful. The best way to avoid burns is to wear rubber gloves or disposable plastic gloves. If you don't have gloves, simply cover your hands with small plastic bags.

If you do happen to get chile oil on your hands, wash them thoroughly with hot, soapy water. Flush your eyes with cool water if they become affected. Finally, clean your knives and cutting boards to keep from transferring chiles' hot oils to other foods.

Ginger-Lemon Pork Chops

Prep: 20 minutes **Marinate:** 4 to 24 hours **Grill:** 11 minutes **Makes:** 4 servings

    4 pork top loin chops, cut 1 inch thick
    ½ cup soy sauce
    ¼ cup water
    1 tablespoon grated fresh ginger
    1 teaspoon finely shredded lemon peel
    1 tablespoon lemon juice

1. Trim fat from chops. Place chops in a resealable plastic bag set in a shallow dish. For marinade, in a bowl combine soy sauce, water, ginger, lemon peel, and lemon juice. Pour over chops; seal bag. Marinate in refrigerator for 4 to 24 hours, turning bag occasionally.

2. Drain chops, discarding marinade. For a charcoal grill, grill chops on the rack of an uncovered grill directly over medium coals for 11 to 13 minutes or until chops are slightly pink in center and juices run clear (160°F), turning once halfway through grilling. (For a gas grill, preheat grill. Reduce heat to medium. Place chops on grill rack over heat. Cover and grill as above.)

Per serving: 257 cal., 9 g total fat (3 g sat. fat), 92 mg chol., 989 mg sodium, 0 g carbo., 0 g fiber, 40 g pro.
Daily Values: 1% vit. A, 4% vit. C, 4% calcium, 7% iron

Cranberry-Chipotle Pork Chops

Cranberry sauce isn't just for Thanksgiving anymore! You'll be thankful for the flavor it lends to pork chops all year long. See photo on page 85.

Prep: 5 minutes **Grill:** 35 minutes **Makes:** 4 servings

  4 pork loin chops, cut 1¼ inches thick

  1 8-ounce can jellied cranberry sauce

  ⅓ cup apricot or peach preserves or apricot or peach spreadable fruit

  ¼ cup chopped onion (optional)

  1 tablespoon lemon juice or cider vinegar

  1 canned chipotle pepper in adobo sauce or 1 fresh jalapeño chile pepper, seeded and chopped

1. Trim fat from chops. For a charcoal grill, arrange medium-hot coals around a drip pan. Test for medium heat above pan. Place chops on grill rack over pan. Cover and grill for 35 to 40 minutes or until chops are slightly pink in center and juices run clear (160°F), turning once halfway through grilling. (For a gas grill, preheat grill. Reduce heat to medium. Adjust for indirect cooking. Grill as above.)

2. Meanwhile, for sauce, in a small saucepan combine cranberry sauce, preserves, onion (if desired), lemon juice, and chipotle pepper. Bring to boiling, stirring constantly; reduce heat. Simmer, uncovered, for 5 minutes, stirring occasionally.

3. To serve, brush chops with some of the sauce; pass remaining sauce.

Per serving: 445 cal., 10 g total fat (4 g sat. fat), 105 mg chol., 113 mg sodium, 39 g carbo., 1 g fiber, 43 g pro.
Daily Values: 1% vit. A, 8% vit. C, 4% calcium, 8% iron

Asian Apricot-Glazed Chops

Don't brush on the glaze too soon; waiting until the last few minutes keeps the apricot preserves from burning.

Prep: 15 minutes **Grill:** 7 minutes **Makes:** 4 servings

⅓ cup apricot preserves

1 tablespoon Oriental chili-garlic sauce

2 teaspoons soy sauce

¼ teaspoon ground ginger

4 boneless pork sirloin chops, cut ¾ inch thick

Salt and black pepper

1. For glaze, place apricot preserves in a small bowl; snip any large pieces of fruit. Stir in chili-garlic sauce, soy sauce, and ginger. Set glaze aside. Sprinkle both sides of chops with salt and pepper.

2. For a charcoal grill, grill chops on the rack of an uncovered grill directly over medium coals for 7 to 9 minutes or until chops are slightly pink in center and juices run clear (160°F), turning once halfway through grilling and brushing with glaze during the last 2 to 3 minutes of grilling. (For a gas grill, preheat grill. Reduce heat to medium. Place chops on grill rack over heat. Cover and grill as above.)

Per serving: 317 cal., 9 g total fat (3 g sat. fat), 106 mg chol., 515 mg sodium, 20 g carbo., 0 g fiber, 36 g pro.
Daily Values: 3% vit. A, 6% vit. C, 3% calcium, 10% iron

Lemon-and-Herb-Rubbed Pork Chops

See photo on page 85.

Prep: 15 minutes **Grill:** 35 minutes **Makes:** 4 servings

  1½ teaspoons finely shredded lemon peel
   1 teaspoon dried rosemary, crushed
   ½ teaspoon salt
   ½ teaspoon dried sage, crushed
   ½ teaspoon black pepper
   8 cloves garlic, minced
   4 pork loin chops, cut 1¼ inches thick

1. For rub, in a small bowl combine lemon peel, rosemary, salt, sage, pepper, and garlic. Trim fat from chops. Sprinkle rub evenly over both sides of chops; rub in with your fingers.

2. For a charcoal grill, arrange medium-hot coals around a drip pan. Test for medium heat above pan. Place chops on grill rack over pan. Cover and grill for 35 to 40 minutes or until chops are slightly pink in center and juices run clear (160°F), turning once halfway through grilling. (For a gas grill, preheat grill. Reduce heat to medium. Adjust for indirect cooking. Grill as above.)

Per serving: 292 cal., 10 g total fat (4 g sat. fat), 105 mg chol., 371 mg sodium, 3 g carbo., 1 g fiber, 43 g pro.
Daily Values: 1% vit. A, 6% vit. C, 5% calcium, 8% iron

Apple Butter Chops

Prep: 10 minutes **Grill:** 11 minutes **Makes:** 4 servings

   4 **pork rib chops, cut ¾ inch thick**
   ½ **teaspoon Kansas City or Montreal steak seasoning**
   ½ **cup bottled chili sauce**
   ¼ **cup apple butter**
   ½ **teaspoon apple pie spice, pumpkin pie spice, or ground cinnamon**

1. Trim fat from chops. Sprinkle both sides of chops lightly with steak seasoning. For sauce, in a bowl combine chili sauce, apple butter, and apple pie spice. Set sauce aside.

2. For a charcoal grill, grill chops on the rack of an uncovered grill directly over medium coals for 11 to 13 minutes or until chops are slightly pink in the center and juices run clear (160°F), turning once halfway through grilling and brushing chops with sauce during the last 5 minutes of grilling. (For a gas grill, preheat grill. Reduce heat to medium. Place chops on grill rack over heat. Cover and grill as above.)

Per serving: 258 cal., 5 g total fat (2 g sat. fat), 47 mg chol., 589 mg sodium, 30 g carbo., 3 g fiber, 20 g pro.
Daily Values: 5% vit. A, 11% vit. C, 4% calcium, 7% iron

Types of Fuel for Charcoal Grills

There are several types of fuel available for charcoal grills. Composition briquettes are a convenient and reliable method for fueling a charcoal grill, but avoid the cheaper brands. They may contain materials such as coal dust, camphor, and paraffin or petroleum binders, which can ruin food's flavor. Natural briquettes made from pulverized lump charcoal tend to impart fewer off-flavors. And better still is charwood or lump charcoal made from hardwoods like maple, oak, and hickory. Because charwood doesn't contain any additives, it cooks cleaner and more natural, though it costs a bit more to use and is less readily available.

Soy-Mustard-Marinated Pork Tenderloins

Prep: 10 minutes **Marinate:** 4 to 6 hours **Grill:** 30 minutes
Stand: 10 minutes **Makes:** 6 servings

  2 12-ounce pork tenderloins
  ½ cup cooking oil
  ⅓ cup soy sauce
  2 tablespoons Worcestershire sauce
  1 tablespoon dry mustard
  ¼ teaspoon black pepper

1. Trim fat from tenderloins. Place tenderloins in a resealable plastic bag set in a shallow dish. For marinade, in a small bowl combine oil, soy sauce, Worcestershire sauce, mustard, and pepper. Pour marinade over tenderloins; seal bag. Marinate in refrigerator for 4 to 6 hours, turning bag occasionally.

2. Drain tenderloins, reserving marinade. For a charcoal grill, arrange hot coals around a drip pan. Test for medium-high heat above pan. Place tenderloins on grill rack over pan. Cover and grill for 30 to 35 minutes or until a meat thermometer registers 155°F, brushing with reserved marinade twice during the first 15 minutes of grilling. Discard any remaining marinade. (For a gas grill, preheat grill. Reduce heat to medium-high. Adjust for indirect cooking. Grill as above.)

3. Remove tenderloins from grill. Cover with foil and let stand 10 minutes before slicing. (The meat's temperature will rise 5°F during standing.)

Per serving: 178 cal., 8 g total fat (2 g sat. fat), 73 mg chol., 264 mg sodium, 0 g carbo., 0 g fiber, 24 g pro.
Daily Values: 2% vit. C, 1% calcium, 7% iron

Peachy Pork Tenderloin

Resting tenderloin after cooking allows the anticipation to build and the delicious juices to distribute evenly as the temperature rises a few degrees.

Prep: 10 minutes **Marinate:** 4 to 24 hours **Grill:** 30 minutes
Stand: 10 minutes **Makes:** 4 servings

> 1 12-ounce pork tenderloin
>
> ⅓ cup peach nectar
>
> 3 tablespoons teriyaki sauce
>
> 2 tablespoons snipped fresh rosemary or 2 teaspoons dried rosemary, crushed
>
> 1 tablespoon olive oil

1. Trim fat from tenderloin. Place tenderloin in a resealable plastic bag set in a shallow dish. For marinade, in a small bowl combine peach nectar, teriyaki sauce, rosemary, and olive oil. Pour marinade over tenderloin; seal bag. Marinate in refrigerator for 4 to 24 hours, turning bag occasionally.

2. Drain tenderloin, discarding marinade. For a charcoal grill, arrange hot coals around a drip pan. Test for medium-high heat above pan. Place tenderloin on grill rack over pan. Cover and grill for 30 to 35 minutes or until a meat thermometer registers 155°F. (For a gas grill, preheat grill. Reduce heat to medium-high. Adjust for indirect cooking. Grill as above.)

3. Remove tenderloin from grill. Cover with foil and let stand 10 minutes before slicing. (The meat's temperature will rise 5°F during standing.)

Per serving: 162 cal., 7 g total fat (2 g sat. fat), 60 mg chol., 285 mg sodium, 6 g carbo., 0 g fiber, 19 g pro.
Daily Values: 2% vit. C, 1% calcium, 8% iron

Pineapple-Glazed Pork

If aloha means goodbye, that's what you'll be saying to this delicious, Hawaiian-inspired pork not long after it hits your plate.

Prep: 10 minutes **Grill:** 30 minutes **Stand:** 10 minutes **Makes:** 6 servings

½ of a 6-ounce can (⅓ cup) frozen pineapple juice concentrate

1 tablespoon Dijon-style mustard

1 teaspoon snipped fresh rosemary or ¼ teaspoon dried rosemary, crushed

1 clove garlic, minced

2 12-ounce pork tenderloins

1. For glaze, in a small saucepan heat juice concentrate, mustard, rosemary, and garlic over medium heat about 5 minutes or until slightly thickened, stirring once. Set glaze aside.

2. Trim fat from tenderloins. For a charcoal grill, arrange hot coals around a drip pan. Test for medium-high heat above pan. Place tenderloins on grill rack over pan. Brush with some of the sauce. Cover and grill for 30 to 35 minutes or until a meat thermometer registers 155°F, brushing again with sauce during the last 10 minutes of grilling. (For a gas grill, preheat grill. Reduce heat to medium-high. Adjust for indirect cooking. Grill as above.)

3. Remove tenderloins from grill. Cover with foil and let stand 10 minutes before slicing. (The meat's temperature will rise 5°F during standing.)

Per serving: 154 cal., 4 g total fat (1 g sat. fat), 81 mg chol., 121 mg sodium, 2 g carbo., 0 g fiber, 25 g pro.
Daily Values: 13% vit. C, 9% iron

Mahogany Glazed Pork

Prep: 15 minutes **Grill:** 12 minutes **Makes:** 4 servings

⅓ cup hoisin sauce

2 tablespoons cider vinegar

½ teaspoon toasted sesame oil

¼ teaspoon black pepper

2 cloves garlic, minced

2 pork shoulder blade steaks, cut ¾ inch thick

1. For glaze, in a small bowl combine hoisin sauce, vinegar, sesame oil, pepper, and garlic. Set glaze aside.

2. For a charcoal grill, grill pork steaks on the rack of an uncovered grill directly over medium coals for 12 to 14 minutes or until steaks are slightly pink in center and juices run clear (160°F), turning once and brushing occasionally with glaze during the last 2 to 3 minutes of grilling. (For a gas grill, preheat grill. Reduce heat to medium. Place steaks on grill rack over heat. Cover and grill as above.)

Per serving: 209 cal., 9 g total fat (3 g sat. fat), 75 mg chol., 342 mg sodium, 7 g carbo., 0 g fiber, 23 g pro.
Daily Values: 3% vit. A, 2% vit. C, 4% calcium, 7% iron

Northern Minnesota Porketta Roast

Porketta is a delicious tradition in northern Minnesota, started by families of Italian descent. There are many secret recipes for this highly seasoned rolled pork shoulder roast, but all contain flavorful fennel seeds.

Prep: 25 minutes **Grill:** 1½ hours **Stand:** 15 minutes **Makes:** 10 to 12 servings

1 3- to 4-pound boneless pork shoulder blade roast (rolled and tied)

½ cup snipped fresh parsley

1½ teaspoons fennel seeds, crushed

1½ teaspoons cracked black pepper

1 teaspoon bottled minced garlic

¾ teaspoon salt

1. Untie pork roast. Trim fat from roast. Using a sharp knife, cut several 1-inch slits all over the roast.

2. For rub, in a small bowl combine parsley, fennel seeds, pepper, garlic, and salt. Press some of the rub into the slits with your fingers. Sprinkle the remaining rub evenly over the entire roast; rub in with your fingers. Retie roast with 100-percent-cotton kitchen string. Insert a meat thermometer into center of roast.

3. For a charcoal grill, arrange medium coals around a drip pan. Test for medium-low heat above pan. Place roast on grill rack over pan. Cover and grill for 1½ to 2¼ hours or until meat thermometer registers 155°F. (For a gas grill, preheat grill. Reduce heat to medium-low. Adjust for indirect cooking. Grill as above.)

4. Remove roast from grill. Cover with foil and let stand for 15 minutes before slicing. (The meat's temperature will rise 5°F during standing.)

Per serving: 208 cal., 10 g total fat (3 g sat. fat), 92 mg chol., 253 mg sodium, 1 g carbo., 0 g fiber, 27 g pro.
Daily Values: 3% vit. A, 9% vit. C, 4% calcium, 11% iron

Rhubarb-Glazed Pork Roast

Prep: 15 minutes **Cook:** 20 minutes **Grill:** 1¼ hours **Stand:** 15 minutes **Makes:** 6 servings

- 2 **cups fresh or frozen sliced rhubarb**
- 1 **6-ounce can (⅔ cup) frozen apple juice concentrate**
  Several drops red food coloring (optional)
- 2 **tablespoons honey**
- 1 **3- to 4-pound pork loin center rib roast, backbone loosened (4 ribs)**

1. For glaze, in a saucepan combine rhubarb, apple juice concentrate, and, if desired, red food coloring. Bring to boiling; reduce heat. Simmer, covered, for 15 to 20 minutes or until rhubarb is very tender. Strain mixture into a small bowl, pressing out liquid with the back of a spoon; discard pulp. Return rhubarb liquid to saucepan. Bring to boiling; reduce heat. Simmer, uncovered, about 5 minutes or until reduced to ½ cup. Remove saucepan from heat; stir in honey. Set aside ¼ cup of the glaze to use for basting. Reserve remaining glaze until ready to serve.

2. Meanwhile, trim fat from roast. Insert a meat thermometer into center of roast without touching bone.

3. For a charcoal grill, arrange medium coals around a drip pan. Test for medium-low heat above pan. Place roast, bone side down, on grill rack over pan. Cover and grill for 1¼ to 2 hours or until thermometer registers 150°F, brushing occasionally with the ¼ cup reserved glaze during the last 15 minutes of grilling. (For a gas grill, preheat grill. Reduce heat to medium-low. Adjust for indirect cooking. Grill as above.)

4. Remove roast from grill. Cover with foil and let stand 15 minutes before slicing. (The meat's temperature will rise 10°F during standing.) Reheat and pass the remaining glaze.

Per serving: 266 cal., 7 g total fat (3 g sat. fat), 71 mg chol., 56 mg sodium, 19 g carbo., 0 g fiber, 29 g pro.
Daily Values: 1% vit. A, 7% vit. C, 7% calcium, 8% iron

Pineapple-Mustard Country-Style Ribs

Country-style ribs are so mouthwateringly good that they need only two ingredients to make a scrumptious sauce.

Prep: 10 minutes **Grill:** 1½ hours **Makes:** 4 servings

½ of a 6-ounce can (⅓ cup) frozen pineapple juice concentrate, thawed

3 tablespoons Dijon-style mustard

2½ to 3 pounds pork country-style ribs

1. For sauce, in a small bowl combine juice concentrate and mustard. Set sauce aside.

2. Trim fat from ribs. For a charcoal grill, arrange medium-hot coals around a drip pan. Test for medium heat above pan. Place ribs, bone sides down, on grill rack over pan. (Or place ribs in a rib rack; place on grill rack.) Cover and grill for 1½ to 2 hours or until ribs are tender, brushing with sauce during the last 10 minutes of grilling. (For a gas grill, preheat grill. Reduce heat to medium. Adjust for indirect cooking. Grill as above.)

Per serving: 296 cal., 12 g total fat (4 g sat. fat), 101 mg chol., 356 mg sodium, 13 g carbo., 0 g fiber, 33 g pro.
Daily Values: 18% vit. C, 6% calcium, 12% iron

Cranberry-Glazed Pork Ribs

Prep: 10 minutes **Grill:** 1½ hours **Makes:** 6 servings

    1 8-ounce can whole cranberry sauce
    3 inches stick cinnamon
    1 tablespoon Dijon-style mustard
    1 teaspoon finely shredded orange peel
  1½ pounds boneless pork country-style ribs

1. For glaze, cook and stir cranberry sauce, stick cinnamon, mustard, and orange peel over medium heat about 5 minutes or until bubbly. Set glaze aside.

2. Trim fat from ribs. For a charcoal grill, arrange medium-hot coals around a drip pan. Test for medium heat above pan. Place ribs on grill rack over pan. (Or place ribs in a rib rack; place on grill rack.) Cover and grill for 1½ to 2 hours or until ribs are tender, brushing occasionally with glaze during the last 20 minutes of grilling. (For a gas grill, preheat grill. Reduce heat to medium. Adjust for indirect cooking. Grill as above.)

3. To serve, reheat any remaining glaze until bubbly. Remove and discard stick cinnamon. Serve glaze with ribs.

Per serving: 255 cal., 14 g total fat (5 g sat. fat), 65 mg chol., 124 mg sodium, 15 g carbo., 0 g fiber, 16 g pro.
Daily Values: 3% vit. C, 1% calcium, 5% iron

Peach-Glazed Baby Back Ribs

Prep: 10 minutes **Grill:** 1½ hours **Makes:** 4 servings

  1 10-ounce jar peach preserves
  2 tablespoons lemon juice
  1 teaspoon Dijon-style mustard
  ¼ teaspoon ground cardamom or ground cinnamon
  4 to 5 pounds pork loin back ribs or meaty pork spareribs
     Salt and black pepper

1. For glaze, in a small saucepan cook and stir peach preserves, lemon juice, mustard, and cardamom over medium heat until preserves melt. Set glaze aside.

2. Trim fat from ribs. Sprinkle ribs with salt and pepper.

3. For a charcoal grill, arrange medium-hot coals around a drip pan. Test for medium heat above pan. Place ribs, bone sides down, on grill rack over drip pan. (Or place ribs in a rib rack; place on grill rack.) Cover and grill for 1½ to 1¾ hours or until ribs are tender, brushing with glaze during the last 15 minutes of grilling. (For a gas grill, preheat grill. Reduce heat to medium. Adjust for indirect cooking. Grill as above.) Serve with any remaining glaze.

Per serving: 644 cal., 19 g total fat (7 g sat. fat), 134 mg chol., 169 mg sodium, 50 g carbo., 1 g fiber, 63 g pro.
Daily Values: 17% vit. C, 4% calcium, 12% iron

Stout-Glazed Ribs

Stout beer glazes the ribs with gorgeous, dark color and deep, rich flavor. The darker the beer, the better the results. See photo on page 85.

Prep: 15 minutes **Marinate:** 6 to 24 hours **Cook:** 10 minutes
Grill: 1½ hours **Makes:** 4 servings

>   4 pounds pork loin back ribs or meaty pork spareribs
>   1 12-ounce bottle stout
>   ½ cup chopped onion
>   ¼ cup honey mustard
>   3 cloves garlic, minced
>   1 teaspoon caraway seeds (optional)
>   Salt and black pepper

1. Trim fat from ribs. Place ribs in resealable plastic bag set in shallow dish. For marinade, in a medium bowl combine stout, onion, honey mustard, garlic, and, if desired, caraway seeds. Pour marinade over ribs; seal bag. Marinate in refrigerator for 6 to 24 hours, turning bag occasionally.

2. Drain ribs, reserving marinade. Sprinkle ribs with salt and pepper. Pour marinade into a small saucepan. Bring to boiling; reduce heat. Simmer, uncovered, for 10 minutes.

3. For a charcoal grill, arrange medium-hot coals around a drip pan. Test for medium heat above pan. Place ribs, bone sides down, on grill rack over drip pan. (Or place ribs in a rib rack; place on grill rack.) Cover and grill for 1½ to 1¾ hours or until ribs are tender, brushing frequently with marinade during the last 10 minutes of grilling. Discard any remaining marinade. (For a gas grill, preheat grill. Adjust for indirect cooking. Grill as above.) If desired, garnish with fresh *sage leaves*.

Per serving: 482 cal., 20 g total fat (7 g sat. fat), 135 mg chol., 296 mg sodium, 5 g carbo., 0 g fiber, 63 g pro.
Daily Values: 3% vit. C, 3% calcium, 13% iron

Maple-and-Mustard-Glazed Ham Steak

Prep: 10 minutes **Grill:** 14 minutes **Makes:** 6 servings

1 1½- to 2-pound cooked center-cut ham slice, cut 1 inch thick
2 tablespoons butter or margarine
¼ cup pure maple syrup or maple-flavored syrup
2 tablespoons brown mustard

1. For a charcoal grill, grill ham on the rack of an uncovered grill directly over medium coals for 14 to 18 minutes or until heated through (140°F). (For a gas grill, preheat grill. Reduce heat to medium. Place ham on grill rack over heat. Cover and grill as above.)

2. Meanwhile, for glaze, in a small saucepan melt butter. Remove saucepan from heat. Stir in syrup and mustard, whisking until smooth. Return saucepan to heat. Bring to boiling; reduce heat. Cook for 1 to 2 minutes more or until slightly thickened.

3. To serve, brush ham with glaze; pass remaining glaze.

Per serving: 258 cal., 14 g total fat (6 g sat. fat), 75 mg chol., 1,575 mg sodium, 14 g carbo., 2 g fiber, 19 g pro.
Daily Values: 2% vit. A, 8% vit. C, 4% calcium, 8% iron

Charcoal Grill Features

Large, kettle-type charcoal grills are often less expensive than gas grills, are able to cook hotter, and do a super job with a wide range of foods. That's why they're a popular choice with many backyard grillmeisters. When looking for a charcoal grill, avoid the small, portable, lidless type because those are designed mainly for direct grilling, not barbecuing with indirect heat.

In a kettle-type grill, look for vents on both top and bottom, which are crucial for controlling the cooking temperature. Also, favor a grill with a heavy, tight-fitting lid and solid construction.

Blackberry-Glazed Ham

All sorts of fruit flavors complement smoky, satisfying ham. This time, blackberry does double duty as both glaze and tangy-sweet sauce.

Prep: 10 minutes **Grill:** 2¼ hours **Makes:** 20 to 28 servings

- 1 6- to 8-pound cooked ham (shank half)
- 1½ cups seedless blackberry jam or other seedless berry jam
- ¼ cup coarse-grain brown mustard
- 2 tablespoons balsamic vinegar

1. Score ham by making diagonal cuts in a diamond pattern at 1-inch intervals. Place ham on a rack in a shallow roasting pan.

2. For sauce, in a medium saucepan combine jam, mustard, and vinegar. Bring just to boiling; reduce heat. Simmer, uncovered, for 5 minutes. Set sauce aside.

3. For a charcoal grill, arrange medium coals around edge of grill. Test for medium-low heat in center of grill. Place roasting pan with ham on grill rack in center of grill. Cover and grill for 2¼ to 2½ hours or until heated through (140°F), brushing once or twice with sauce during the last 15 minutes of grilling. (For a gas grill, preheat grill. Reduce heat to medium-low. Adjust for indirect cooking. Grill as above.)

4. To serve, slice ham. Reheat any remaining sauce until bubbly; pass with ham.

Per serving: 238 cal., 9 g total fat (3 g sat. fat), 58 mg chol., 1,380 mg sodium, 21 g carbo., 2 g fiber, 17 g pro.
Daily Values: 10% vit. C, 3% calcium, 7% iron

Honeyed Ham on the Grill

Prep: 20 minutes **Grill:** 70 minutes **Makes:** 12 to 16 servings

  1 **5- to 6-pound cooked ham (shank half)**
  ½ **cup honey**
  2 **tablespoons steak sauce**
  ½ **teaspoon dry mustard**

1. Have your butcher trim the fat and remove the bone from the ham. Discard the ham bone or save it for another use.

2. Center the ham on a piece of heavy foil that's large enough to wrap around the ham. Combine the honey, steak sauce, and mustard. Pour half of the honey mixture over the ham and into the cavity left by the bone. Bring up two opposite edges of the foil and seal with a double fold. Fold the remaining edges together to completely enclose the ham, leaving space for steam to build. Place the foil-wrapped ham on a rack in a shallow roasting pan.

3. For a charcoal grill, arrange medium coals around edge of grill. Test for medium-low heat in center of grill. Place roasting pan with ham on grill rack in center of grill. Cover and grill for 30 minutes. Carefully fold back foil at top of ham and pour the remaining honey mixture over ham. Reseal the foil. Cover and grill about 30 minutes more or until heated through (140°F). Fold back foil at top of ham. Cover and grill 10 minutes more. (For a gas grill, preheat grill. Reduce heat to medium-low. Adjust for indirect cooking. Grill as above.)

Per serving: 353 cal., 16 g total fat (6 g sat. fat), 108 mg chol., 2,504 mg sodium, 19 g carbo., 3 g fiber, 31 g pro.
Daily Values: 13% vit. C, 5% calcium, 11% iron

poultry

Garlicky Grilled Chicken

Sprinkled liberally with ground coffee, this tasty grilled chicken can double as a pick-me-up!

Prep: 15 minutes **Grill:** 1 hour **Stand:** 10 minutes **Makes:** 4 servings

1 2½- to 3-pound whole broiler-fryer chicken
1 tablespoon cooking oil
2 cloves garlic, minced
1 teaspoon dark roast ground coffee
   Salt and black pepper

1. Remove the neck and giblets from chicken. Skewer neck skin to back. Tie legs to tail. Twist wing tips under back. In a small bowl combine oil and garlic. Brush garlic mixture over chicken; sprinkle with coffee, salt, and pepper.

2. For a charcoal grill, arrange medium-hot coals around a drip pan. Test for medium heat above pan. Place chicken, breast side up, on grill rack over drip pan. Cover and grill 1 to 1¼ hours or until chicken is no longer pink and drumsticks move easily (180°F in thigh muscle). (For a gas grill, preheat grill. Reduce heat to medium. Adjust for indirect cooking. Grill as above.)

3. Remove chicken from grill. Cover with foil and let stand for 10 minutes before carving.

Per serving: 462 cal., 34 g total fat (9 g sat. fat), 148 mg chol., 402 mg sodium, 1 g carbo., 0 g fiber, 35 g pro.
Daily Values: 4% vit. A, 1% vit. C, 2% calcium, 11% iron

Honey-Dijon Barbecued Chicken

See photo on page 86.

Prep: 15 minutes **Marinate:** 8 to 24 hours **Grill:** 50 minutes **Makes:** 4 servings

  1 2½- to 3-pound broiler-fryer chicken, quartered
  ½ cup white Zinfandel wine or apple juice
  ½ cup honey mustard
  ¼ cup olive oil
  ½ teaspoon black pepper
  ¼ teaspoon salt
  4 cloves garlic, minced

1. Place chicken in a resealable plastic bag set in a shallow dish. For marinade, in a medium bowl combine wine, honey mustard, oil, pepper, salt, and garlic. Pour marinade over chicken; seal bag. Marinate in refrigerator 8 to 24 hours, turning bag occasionally.

2. Drain chicken, reserving marinade. For a charcoal grill, arrange medium-hot coals around a drip pan. Test for medium heat above pan. Place chicken quarters, bone sides up, on grill rack over drip pan. Cover and grill for 50 to 60 minutes or until chicken is no longer pink (170°F for breast portions; 180°F for drumstick portions), turning once halfway through grilling and brushing once with reserved marinade after 30 minutes of grilling. (For a gas grill, preheat grill. Reduce heat to medium. Adjust for indirect cooking. Grill as above.) Discard any remaining marinade.

Per serving: 530 cal., 39 g total fat (11 g sat. fat), 149 mg chol., 302 mg sodium, 4 g carbo., 0 g fiber, 35 g pro.
Daily Values: 5% vit. A, 1% vit. C, 2% calcium, 12% iron

Garlic-Rubbed Chicken

Putting this luscious garlic and basil rub under the skin gets the good stuff right where you want it—next to the meat.

Prep: 20 minutes **Grill:** 1 hour **Stand:** 10 minutes **Makes:** 5 servings

- 1   2½- to 3-pound whole broiler-fryer chicken
- 3   cloves garlic, peeled
- 1   teaspoon dried basil, crushed
- ⅛   teaspoon salt
- 1   tablespoon cooking oil
- 1   tablespoon lemon juice

1. Remove the neck and giblets from chicken. Twist wing tips under the back. Cut one of the garlic cloves in half lengthwise. Rub the skin of the chicken with the cut edges of the garlic; discard garlic halves. Mince the remaining 2 cloves of garlic. Combine the minced garlic, basil, and salt; set aside.

2. Starting at the neck on one side of the breast, slip your fingers between the skin and meat, loosening the skin as you work toward the tail end. Once your entire hand is under the skin, free the skin around the thigh and leg area up to, but not around, the tip of the drumstick. Repeat on the other side of the breast. Rub the garlic mixture under skin over the entire surface. Skewer the neck skin to the back. Stir together the oil and lemon juice; brush some of the oil mixture over the chicken.

3. For a charcoal grill, arrange medium-hot coals around a drip pan. Test for medium heat above pan. Place chicken, breast side up, on grill rack over drip pan. Cover and grill 1 to 1¼ hours or until chicken is no longer pink and drumsticks move easily (180°F in thigh muscle), brushing occasionally with the remaining oil mixture. (For a gas grill, preheat grill. Reduce heat to medium. Adjust for indirect cooking. Grill as above.)

4. Remove chicken from grill. Cover with foil and let stand for 10 minutes before carving.

Per serving: 505 cal., 37 g total fat (10 g sat. fat), 164 mg chol., 182 mg sodium, 1 g carbo., 0 g fiber, 39 g pro.
Daily Values: 5% vit. A, 3% vit. C, 3% calcium, 12% iron

Gremolata Rotisserie Chicken

Prep: 40 minutes **Grill:** 1 hour **Stand:** 10 minutes **Makes:** 8 to 10 servings

½ cup butter, softened

3 tablespoons finely chopped fresh parsley

1 tablespoon minced garlic

1 tablespoon finely shredded lemon peel

2 3- to 3½-pound whole broiler-fryer chickens

1. For gremolata butter, in a small bowl combine butter, parsley, garlic, lemon peel, and, if desired, 1 finely chopped *anchovy fillet*; set aside.

2. Remove the neck and giblets from chickens. Starting at the neck on one side of the breast, slip your fingers between skin and meat, loosening the skin as you work toward the tail end. Once your entire hand is under the skin, free the skin around the thigh and leg area up to, but not around, the tip of the drumstick. Repeat on the other side of the breast. Rub half of the gremolata butter under the skin over the entire surface. Skewer the neck skin to the back. Repeat with remaining chicken. Sprinkle surfaces and cavities of both chickens with *salt* and *pepper.*

3. To secure chickens on a spit rod, place one holding fork on rod, tines toward point. Insert rod through one of the chickens, neck end first, pressing tines of holding fork firmly into breast meat. To tie wings, slip a 24-inch piece of 100-percent-cotton kitchen string under back of chicken; bring ends of string to front, looping around each wing tip. Tie in center of breast, leaving equal string ends. To tie legs, slip a 24-inch piece of string under tail. Loop string around tail, then around crossed legs. Tie very tightly to hold bird securely on spit, again leaving string ends. Pull together the strings attached to wings and legs; tie tightly. Trim excess string. Place second holding fork on rod, tines toward the chicken; press tines of holding fork firmly into thigh meat. Adjust forks and tighten screws. Repeat with remaining chicken on the same rod. Test balance, making adjustments as necessary.

4. For a charcoal grill, arrange medium-hot coals around a drip pan. Test for medium heat above the pan. Attach spit; turn on the motor and lower the grill hood. Let the chickens rotate over drip pan for 1 to 1¼ hours or until chicken is no longer pink and drumsticks move easily (180°F in thigh muscle). (For a gas grill, preheat grill, reduce heat to medium. Adjust for indirect cooking. Grill as above.)

5. Remove chickens from spit. Cover with foil and let stand for 10 minutes before carving.

Per serving: 621 cal., 49 g total fat (18 g sat. fat), 208 mg chol., 216 mg sodium, 1 g carbo., 0 g fiber, 42 g pro.
Daily Values: 14% vit. A, 6% vit. C, 3% calcium, 13% iron

Guava-Glazed Chicken

Prep: 20 minutes **Cook:** 15 minutes **Grill:** 45 minutes **Stand:** 10 minutes **Makes:** 6 servings

  1 **3- to 4-pound whole broiler-fryer chicken**

  ½ **teaspoon salt**

  ¼ **teaspoon black pepper**

  1 **cup guava, peach, or apricot nectar**

  ¼ **cup bottled hoisin sauce**

  2 **cloves garlic, minced**

    Several dashes bottled hot pepper sauce (optional)

1. Remove the neck and giblets from chicken. Place chicken, breast side down, on a cutting board. Use kitchen shears to make a lengthwise cut down one side of the backbone, starting from the neck end. Repeat the lengthwise cut on the opposite side of the backbone. Remove and discard the backbone. Turn chicken cut side down. Flatten the chicken as much as possible with your hands. Use kitchen shears to remove the wing tips. Sprinkle chicken with salt and pepper.

2. For sauce, in a small saucepan combine nectar, hoisin sauce, garlic, and, if desired, hot pepper sauce. Bring to boiling; reduce heat. Boil gently, uncovered, about 15 minutes or until sauce is thickened and reduced to about ¾ cup. Set sauce aside.

3. For a charcoal grill, grill chicken, bone side up, on the rack of an uncovered grill directly over medium coals for 45 to 50 minutes or until chicken is no longer pink (180°F in thigh muscle), turning once halfway through grilling and brushing with some of the sauce during the last 5 minutes of grilling. (For a gas grill, preheat grill. Reduce heat to medium. Place chicken on grill rack over heat. Cover and grill as above.)

4. Remove chicken from grill. Cover with foil and let stand 10 minutes before carving.

5. Meanwhile, bring the remaining sauce to boiling; pass with chicken.

Per serving: 272 cal., 12 g total fat (3 g sat. fat), 79 mg chol., 478 mg sodium, 13 g carbo., 0 g fiber, 25 g pro.
Daily Values: 12% vit. C, 2% calcium, 7% iron

Herb-Rubbed Chicken

Prep: 10 minutes **Grill:** 35 minutes **Makes:** 6 servings

- ½ teaspoon salt
- ½ teaspoon dried thyme, crushed
- ½ teaspoon dried rosemary, crushed
- ½ teaspoon dried savory, crushed
- ¼ teaspoon black pepper
- 2½ to 3 pounds meaty chicken pieces (breast halves, thighs, and drumsticks)

1. For rub, in a small bowl combine salt, thyme, rosemary, savory, and pepper. Sprinkle rub evenly over chicken; rub in with your fingers.

2. For a charcoal grill, grill chicken, bone sides up, on the greased rack of an uncovered grill directly over medium coals for 35 to 45 minutes or until chicken is no longer pink (170°F for breasts; 180°F for thighs and drumsticks), turning once halfway through grilling. (For a gas grill, preheat grill. Reduce heat to medium. Place chicken on greased grill rack over heat. Cover and grill as above.)

Per serving: 202 cal., 10 g total fat (3 g sat. fat), 81 mg chol., 265 mg sodium, 0 g carbo., 0 g fiber, 26 g pro.
Daily Values: 1% vit. A, 2% calcium, 7% iron

Hot Barbecued Chicken

This spicy chicken marinade is so blazingly hot, you might not need any matches to fire up your grill.

Prep: 10 minutes **Marinate:** 2 to 3 hours **Grill:** 50 minutes **Makes:** 6 servings

2½ to 3 pounds meaty chicken pieces (breast halves, thighs, and drumsticks)
1 2-ounce bottle (¼ cup) hot pepper sauce
3 tablespoons ketchup
3 tablespoons Worcestershire sauce

1. Place chicken pieces in a resealable plastic bag set in a shallow dish. For marinade, combine hot pepper sauce, ketchup, and Worcestershire sauce. Pour over chicken pieces; seal bag. Marinate in refrigerator for 2 to 3 hours, turning bag occasionally.

2. Drain chicken, discarding marinade. For a charcoal grill, arrange medium-hot coals around a drip pan. Test for medium heat above pan. Place chicken pieces, bone sides up, on grill rack over drip pan. Cover and grill for 50 to 60 minutes or until chicken is no longer pink (170°F for breasts; 180°F for thighs and drumsticks), turning once halfway through grilling. (For a gas grill, preheat grill. Reduce heat to medium. Adjust for indirect cooking. Grill as above.)

Per serving: 285 cal., 17 g total fat (5 g sat. fat), 110 mg chol., 201 mg sodium, 2 g carbo., 0 g fiber, 29 g pro.
Daily Values: 5% vit. A, 6% vit. C, 2% calcium, 8% iron

Pesto Chicken

Prep: 10 minutes **Grill:** 50 minutes **Makes:** 4 servings

    1 tablespoon olive oil

    4 cloves garlic, minced

2½ to 3 pounds meaty chicken pieces (breast halves, thighs, and drumsticks)

    2 tablespoons purchased basil pesto

    1 recipe Pesto Butter (page 186)

1. In a small bowl combine oil and garlic; brush chicken pieces with oil mixture.

2. For a charcoal grill, arrange medium-hot coals around a drip pan. Test for medium heat above pan. Place chicken pieces, bone sides up, on grill rack over drip pan. Cover and grill for 50 to 60 minutes or until chicken is no longer pink (170°F for breasts; 180°F for thighs and drumsticks), turning once halfway through grilling and brushing with purchased pesto during the last 5 minutes of grilling. (For a gas grill, preheat grill. Reduce heat to medium. Adjust for indirect cooking. Grill as above.)

3. To serve, remove chicken from grill. Immediately spread Pesto Butter over chicken pieces.

Per serving: 567 cal., 40 g total fat (12 g sat. fat), 157 mg chol., 339 mg sodium, 5 g carbo., 1 g fiber, 45 g pro.
Daily Values: 7% vit. A, 2% vit. C, 7% calcium, 11% iron

Sweet and Smoky Chicken

Prep: 15 minutes **Grill:** 50 minutes **Makes:** 4 servings

2½ to 3 pounds chicken breast halves and thighs
½ cup vinegar
⅓ cup packed brown sugar
2 tablespoons Worcestershire sauce
¾ teaspoon liquid smoke
½ teaspoon salt
¼ teaspoon black pepper

1. If desired, remove skin from chicken. For sauce, in a small saucepan combine vinegar, brown sugar, Worcestershire sauce, liquid smoke, salt, and pepper. Bring to boiling; reduce heat. Simmer, uncovered, for 5 to 8 minutes or until sauce is reduced to ⅔ cup.

2. For a charcoal grill, arrange medium-hot coals around a drip pan. Test for medium heat above pan. Place chicken, bone sides up, on grill rack over drip pan. Cover and grill for 50 to 60 minutes or until chicken is no longer pink (170°F for breast halves; 180°F for thighs), turning once halfway through grilling and brushing with sauce during the last 15 minutes of grilling. (For a gas grill, preheat grill. Reduce heat to medium. Adjust for indirect cooking. Grill as above.)

Per serving: 245 cal., 4 g total fat (1 g sat. fat), 94 mg chol., 483 mg sodium, 22 g carbo., 0 g fiber, 29 g pro.
Daily Values: 1% vit. A, 3% calcium, 14% iron

Flavor Is More Than Skin Deep

We've all heard that removing the skin from chicken and turkey greatly reduces fat. But that doesn't mean you need to remove it before grilling. In fact, leaving the skin on while grilling—but removing it just before serving—helps the meat stay moist and flavorful while not adding significant fat.

Kickin' Chicken

Are you makin' this finger-lickin' Kickin' Chicken? Clock's tickin'!

Prep: 20 minutes **Grill:** 50 minutes **Makes:** 4 servings

2½ to 3 pounds meaty chicken pieces (breast halves, thighs, and drumsticks)
   Salt and black pepper
⅔ cup orange marmalade
¼ cup bottled chili sauce
2 tablespoons soy sauce
1 tablespoon ground coriander (optional)
¼ teaspoon bottled hot pepper sauce

1. If desired, remove skin from chicken. Sprinkle chicken with salt and pepper.

2. For sauce, in a small saucepan combine marmalade, chili sauce, soy sauce, coriander (if desired), and hot pepper sauce. Cook over medium heat just until bubbly, stirring occasionally. Set aside ⅓ cup of the sauce to use for basting. Reserve remaining sauce until ready to serve.

3. For a charcoal grill, arrange medium-hot coals around a drip pan. Test for medium heat above pan. Place chicken, bone sides up, over drip pan. Cover and grill for 50 to 60 minutes or until chicken is no longer pink (170°F for breasts; 180°F for thighs and drumsticks), turning once halfway through grilling and brushing with basting sauce during the last 10 minutes of grilling. (For a gas grill, preheat grill. Reduce heat to medium. Adjust for indirect cooking. Grill as above.)

4. Serve chicken pieces with reserved sauce.

Per serving: 474 cal., 16 g total fat (4 g sat. fat), 130 mg chol., 952 mg sodium, 39 g carbo., 1 g fiber, 43 g pro.
Daily Values: 3% vit. A, 9% vit. C, 5% calcium, 11% iron

Orange-Coriander-Glazed Chicken

See photo on page 87.

Prep: 30 minutes **Grill:** 50 minutes **Makes:** 4 servings

⅓ cup orange marmalade

1 tablespoon soy sauce

1 tablespoon Oriental chili sauce

1½ teaspoons ground coriander

2½ to 3 pounds meaty chicken pieces (breast halves, thighs, and drumsticks)

Salt and black pepper

Orange wedges (optional)

1. For glaze, in a small saucepan combine marmalade, soy sauce, chili sauce, and coriander. Heat and stir over low heat until marmalade melts. Set glaze aside.

2. If desired, remove skin from chicken. Sprinkle chicken with salt and pepper. For a charcoal grill, arrange medium-hot coals around a drip pan. Test for medium heat above pan. Place chicken pieces, bone sides up, on grill rack over pan. Cover and grill 50 to 60 minutes or until chicken is no longer pink (170°F for breasts; 180°F for thighs and drumsticks), turning once halfway through grilling and brushing occasionally with glaze during the last 10 minutes of grilling. (For a gas grill, preheat grill. Reduce heat to medium. Adjust for indirect cooking. Cover and grill as above.)

3. If desired, serve chicken with orange wedges.

Per serving: 400 cal., 16 g total fat (4 g sat. fat), 130 mg chol., 554 mg sodium, 20 g carbo., 1 g fiber, 42 g pro.
Daily Values: 1% vit. A, 2% vit. C, 4% calcium, 11% iron

Chicken with Lemon Thyme Pesto

This creative spin on pesto combines pistachios and lemon thyme instead of traditional basil and pine nuts.

Prep: 1 hour **Grill:** 50 minutes **Makes:** 6 servings

  3½ pounds meaty chicken pieces (breast halves, thighs, and drumsticks)
       Salt and black pepper
  1⅓ cups fresh lemon thyme
  ½   cup salted pistachio nuts
  ½   cup olive oil
  ¼   teaspoon black pepper
       Lemon wedges

1. If desired, remove skin from chicken. Season with salt and pepper.

2. For pesto, in a food processor or blender combine lemon thyme and pistachios. Cover and process or blend with several on/off turns until finely chopped. With processor or blender running, gradually drizzle in oil, stopping to scrape down sides as necessary. Stir in the ¼ teaspoon pepper. Set pesto aside.

3. For a charcoal grill, arrange medium-hot coals around a drip pan. Test for medium heat above pan. Place chicken pieces, bone sides up, on grill rack over drip pan. Cover and grill for 50 to 60 minutes or until chicken is no longer pink (170°F for breasts; 180°F for thighs and drumsticks), turning once halfway through grilling and brushing with half of the pesto during the last 5 minutes of grilling. (For a gas grill, preheat grill. Reduce heat to medium. Adjust for indirect cooking. Grill as above.)

4. Cover and chill remaining pesto for another use. Serve chicken with lemon wedges.

Per serving: 414 cal., 26 g total fat (6 g sat. fat), 121 mg chol., 225 mg sodium, 3 g carbo., 1 g fiber, 40 g pro.
Daily Values: 5% vit. A, 12% vit. C, 4% calcium, 15% iron

Chipotle-Peach-Glazed Chicken Thighs

A tiny amount of nutmeg can make a dish come alive even when its flavor is so subtle you hardly know it's there. See photo on page 87.

Prep: 20 minutes **Grill:** 50 minutes **Makes:** 4 servings

  8 chicken thighs
  ½ teaspoon salt
  ¼ teaspoon black pepper
  ¼ teaspoon ground nutmeg
  ⅓ cup peach preserves
  2 tablespoons white wine vinegar
  2 to 3 teaspoons chopped canned chipotle peppers in adobo sauce

1. Remove skin from chicken. For rub, combine salt, black pepper, and half of the nutmeg. Sprinkle rub evenly over chicken thighs; rub in with your fingers.

2. For glaze, in a small saucepan combine remaining nutmeg, peach preserves, vinegar, and chipotle pepper. Cook and stir just until preserves melt. Set glaze aside.

3. For a charcoal grill, arrange medium-hot coals around a drip pan. Test for medium heat above pan. Place chicken, bone sides up, on grill rack over drip pan. Cover and grill for 50 to 60 minutes or until chicken is no longer pink (180°F), brushing with glaze during the last 10 minutes of grilling. (For a gas grill, preheat grill. Reduce heat to medium. Adjust for indirect cooking. Grill as above.)

Per serving: 462 cal., 27 g total fat (8 g sat. fat), 157 mg chol., 426 mg sodium, 18 g carbo., 0 g fiber, 33 g pro.
Daily Values: 5% vit. A, 10% vit. C, 2% calcium, 11% iron

Buttermilk-Soaked Chicken Thighs

Down-home cooks have long known that a dip in buttermilk is the secret for preparing tender, succulent chicken.

Prep: 15 minutes **Marinate:** 4 to 6 hours **Grill:** 50 minutes **Makes:** 4 servings

    8 chicken thighs
    ¾ cup buttermilk
    3 tablespoons snipped fresh chives
    1 tablespoon finely shredded lemon peel (optional)
    3 tablespoons lemon juice
    3 cloves garlic, minced

1. If desired, remove skin from chicken. Place chicken in a resealable plastic bag set in a shallow dish. For marinade, combine buttermilk, chives, lemon peel (if desired), lemon juice, and garlic. Pour over chicken; seal bag. Marinate in refrigerator for 4 to 6 hours, turning bag occasionally.

2. Drain chicken, discarding marinade. For a charcoal grill, arrange medium-hot coals around a drip pan. Test for medium heat above pan. Place chicken, bone sides up, on grill rack over drip pan. Cover and grill for 50 to 60 minutes or until chicken is no longer pink (180°F), turning once halfway through grilling. (For a gas grill, preheat grill. Reduce heat to medium. Adjust for indirect cooking. Grill as above.)

Per serving: 556 cal., 39 g total fat (11 g sat. fat), 224 mg chol., 180 mg sodium, 2 g carbo., 0 g fiber, 47 g pro.
Daily Values: 7% vit. A, 20% vit. C, 5% calcium, 14% iron

Chicken Italiano

Prep: 15 minutes **Marinate:** 8 to 24 hours **Grill:** 50 minutes **Makes:** 4 to 6 servings

  4 to 6 chicken breast halves

1½ cups dry white wine

  ½ cup olive oil or cooking oil

  1 tablespoon dried Italian seasoning, crushed

  2 teaspoons bottled minced garlic

1. If desired, remove skin from chicken. Place chicken in a resealable plastic bag set in a shallow dish. For marinade, combine wine, oil, Italian seasoning, and garlic. Pour over chicken; seal bag. Marinate in refrigerator for 8 to 24 hours, turning bag occasionally.

2. Drain chicken, reserving marinade. For a charcoal grill, arrange medium-hot coals around a drip pan. Test for medium heat above pan. Place chicken, bone sides up, on grill rack over drip pan. Cover and grill for 50 to 60 minutes or until chicken is no longer pink (170°F), turning and brushing once with reserved marinade halfway through grilling. (For a gas grill, preheat grill. Reduce heat to medium. Adjust for indirect cooking. Grill as above.)

Per serving: 462 cal., 29 g total fat (7 g sat. fat), 135 mg chol., 108 mg sodium, 1 g carbo., 0 g fiber, 41 g pro.
Daily Values: 3% vit. A, 1% vit. C, 3% calcium, 10% iron

Balsamic Barbecued Chicken Breasts

Make a double batch of this supereasy, all-around-tasty sauce and refrigerate the rest to try later with pork or burgers.

Prep: 15 minutes **Grill:** 12 minutes **Makes:** 4 servings

½ cup ketchup

¼ cup light-colored corn syrup

3 tablespoons balsamic vinegar or cider vinegar

2 tablespoons thinly sliced green onion

Several dashes bottled hot pepper sauce (optional)

4 skinless, boneless chicken breast halves

1. For sauce, in a small saucepan combine ketchup, corn syrup, vinegar, green onion, and, if desired, hot pepper sauce. Bring to boiling; reduce heat. Simmer, uncovered, 5 to 10 minutes or until desired consistency, stirring sauce occasionally.

2. For a charcoal grill, grill chicken on the rack of an uncovered grill directly over medium coals for 12 to 15 minutes or until chicken is no longer pink (170°F), turning once halfway through grilling and brushing often with sauce during the last 10 minutes of grilling. (For a gas grill, preheat grill. Reduce heat to medium. Place chicken on grill rack over heat. Cover and grill as above.)

3. To serve, reheat any remaining sauce until bubbly; serve with chicken.

Per serving: 267 cal., 2 g total fat (1 g sat. fat), 82 mg chol., 432 mg sodium, 27 g carbo., 0 g fiber, 33 g pro.
Daily Values: 7% vit. A, 9% vit. C, 3% calcium, 7% iron

Shanghai Chicken Breasts

Prep: 10 minutes **Marinate:** 2 to 24 hours **Grill:** 12 minutes **Makes:** 8 servings

  8 skinless, boneless chicken breast halves
½ cup bottled oil-and-vinegar salad dressing
  3 tablespoons soy sauce
  2 tablespoons bottled hoisin sauce
½ teaspoon ground ginger
     Bottled hoisin sauce (optional)

1. Place chicken breasts in a resealable plastic bag. For marinade, combine salad dressing, soy sauce, the 2 tablespoons hoisin sauce, and ginger. Pour over chicken; seal bag. Marinate in refrigerator for 2 to 24 hours, turning bag occasionally.

2. Drain chicken, discarding marinade. For a charcoal grill, grill chicken on the rack of an uncovered grill directly over medium coals for 12 to 15 minutes or until chicken is no longer pink (170°F), turning once halfway through grilling. (For a gas grill, preheat grill. Reduce heat to medium. Place chicken on grill rack over heat. Cover and grill as above.)

3. If desired, serve chicken with additional hoisin sauce.

Per serving: 189 cal., 5 g total fat (1 g sat. fat), 82 mg chol., 286 mg sodium, 1 g carbo., 0 g fiber, 33 g pro.
Daily Values: 1% vit. A, 2% vit. C, 2% calcium, 5% iron

Tangy Lemon Chicken

See photo on page 88.

Prep: 10 minutes **Marinate:** 2 to 4 hours **Grill:** 12 minutes **Makes:** 4 servings

    4 skinless, boneless chicken breast halves
    ½ cup bottled creamy Italian salad dressing
    1 tablespoon finely shredded lemon peel
    ¼ cup lemon juice
       Dash black pepper
       Torn mixed salad greens (optional)

1. Place chicken in a resealable plastic bag. For marinade, in a small bowl combine salad dressing, lemon peel, lemon juice, and pepper. Pour over chicken; seal bag. Marinate in refrigerator for 2 to 4 hours, turning bag occasionally.

2. Drain chicken, reserving marinade. For a charcoal grill, grill chicken on the rack of an uncovered grill directly over medium coals for 12 to 15 minutes until chicken is no longer pink (170°F), turning once and brushing with reserved marinade halfway through grilling. (For a gas grill, preheat grill. Reduce heat to medium. Place chicken on grill rack over heat. Cover and grill as above.) If desired, slice chicken and serve on salad greens.

Per serving: 233 cal., 12 g total fat (2 g sat. fat), 66 mg chol., 302 mg sodium, 4 g carbo., 0 g fiber, 26 g pro.
Daily Values: 1% vit. A, 15% vit. C, 2% calcium, 4% iron

Chicken with Salsa

You can't ask for a quicker, better grilling recipe than this. It clocks in at 22 minutes from start to finish.

Prep: 10 minutes **Grill:** 12 minutes **Makes:** 4 servings

  1 tablespoon cooking oil
  1 teaspoon chili powder
  ¾ teaspoon salt
  4 skinless, boneless chicken breast halves
  ½ cup hot-style thick-and-chunky salsa
  1 tablespoon tomato paste

1. In a small bowl combine oil, chili powder, and salt; brush onto chicken breast halves.

2. In a blender or food processor combine salsa and tomato paste. Cover and blend until nearly smooth.

3. For a charcoal grill, grill chicken on the rack of an uncovered grill directly over medium coals for 12 to 15 minutes or until chicken is no longer pink (170°F), turning once halfway through grilling and brushing often with salsa mixture during the last 2 minutes of grilling. (For a gas grill, preheat grill. Reduce heat to medium. Place chicken on grill rack over heat. Cover and grill as above.)

Per serving: 207 cal., 6 g total fat (1 g sat. fat), 82 mg chol., 752 mg sodium, 3 g carbo., 0 g fiber, 33 g pro.
Daily Values: 6% vit. A, 2% vit. C, 2% calcium, 6% iron

Chicken with Pineapple-Hoisin Glaze

Never turn your back on a slice of pineapple when it's on the grill! Pineapple burns oh so easily if you're not vigilant.

Prep: 25 minutes **Grill:** 12 minutes **Makes:** 4 servings

    1 20-ounce can pineapple slices (juice pack), drained
    3 tablespoons bottled hoisin sauce
    ⅛ to ¼ teaspoon crushed red pepper
    4 skinless, boneless chicken breast halves
    2 tablespoons snipped fresh cilantro

1. For glaze, remove and reserve 4 slices of pineapple. Chop the remaining pineapple slices (you should have about 1¼ cups). In a blender or small food processor combine the chopped pineapple, hoisin sauce, and crushed red pepper. Cover and blend until nearly smooth.

2. For a charcoal grill, grill chicken on the rack of an uncovered grill directly over medium coals for 12 to 15 minutes or until chicken is no longer pink (170°F), turning once and brushing with half of the glaze halfway through grilling. After 6 minutes of grilling, add pineapple slices to grill rack; brush with glaze. (For a gas grill, preheat grill. Reduce heat to medium. Place chicken and pineapple on grill rack over heat. Cover and grill as above.)

3. Reheat remaining glaze until bubbly; serve with chicken and pineapple. Sprinkle with cilantro.

Per serving: 268 cal., 3 g total fat (1 g sat. fat), 82 mg chol., 235 mg sodium, 27 g carbo., 2 g fiber, 34 g pro.
Daily Values: 12% vit. A, 24% vit. C, 5% calcium, 8% iron

Pesto Chicken and Pepper Packets

Prep: 45 minutes **Grill:** 20 minutes **Makes:** 4 servings

    4 skinless, boneless chicken breast halves
    2 medium red, yellow, and/or green sweet peppers, cut into ½-inch-wide strips (2 cups)
    1 small onion, thinly sliced and separated into rings
    ¾ cup purchased basil pesto
    ¼ cup pine nuts, toasted

1. Place each chicken breast half between 2 pieces of plastic wrap. Using the flat side of a meat mallet, pound chicken lightly to about ½-inch thickness. Remove plastic wrap.

2. Tear off four 24×18-inch pieces of heavy foil; fold each in half to make 18×12-inch rectangles. Arrange sweet pepper strips and onion rings in the center of each foil rectangle. Top each with a chicken breast half. Spread pesto evenly over chicken; sprinkle with pine nuts. Bring up two opposite edges of foil and seal with a double fold. Fold remaining edges together to completely enclose mixture, leaving space for steam to build.

3. For a charcoal grill, grill packets on the rack of an uncovered grill directly over medium coals about 20 minutes or until chicken is no longer pink (170°F), turning packets once halfway through grilling (carefully open one packet to check doneness). (For a gas grill, preheat grill. Reduce heat to medium. Place packets on grill rack over heat. Cover and grill as above.)

Per serving: 559 cal., 38 g total fat (1 g sat. fat), 88 mg chol., 427 mg sodium, 15 g carbo., 1 g fiber, 42 g pro.
Daily Values: 36% vit. A, 162% vit. C, 3% calcium, 12% iron

Chicken Burgundy

Adorn tried-and-true chicken breast with an upscale burgundy and marmalade sauce and it becomes fare worthy of any occasion.

Prep: 10 minutes **Grill:** 12 minutes **Makes:** 4 servings

⅓ cup orange marmalade

¼ cup burgundy or other dry red wine

¼ teaspoon salt

4 skinless, boneless chicken breast halves

1. For sauce, in a small saucepan combine orange marmalade, burgundy, and salt. Cook and stir over low heat until marmalade melts. Remove from heat. Set sauce aside.

2. For a charcoal grill, grill chicken on the rack of an uncovered grill directly over medium coals for 12 to 15 minutes or until chicken is no longer pink (170°), turning once halfway through grilling and brushing with some of the sauce during the last 5 minutes of grilling. (For a gas grill, preheat grill. Reduce heat to medium. Place chicken on grill rack over heat. Cover and grill as above.)

3. To serve, reheat remaining sauce until bubbly; serve with chicken.

Per serving: 239 cal., 2 g total fat (1 g sat. fat), 82 mg chol., 237 mg sodium, 18 g carbo., 0 g fiber, 33 g pro.
Daily Values: 1% vit. A, 2% vit. C, 3% calcium, 5% iron

Garlic-Balsamic-Marinated Chicken Breasts

Prep: 15 minutes **Marinate:** 4 to 24 hours **Grill:** 8 minutes **Makes:** 4 servings

    4 skinless, boneless chicken breast halves
    ¼ cup balsamic vinegar
    ¼ cup olive oil
    3 cloves garlic, minced
    ¼ teaspoon crushed red pepper
    ¼ teaspoon salt
    ¼ teaspoon black pepper

1. Place each chicken breast half between 2 pieces of plastic wrap. Using the flat side of a meat mallet, pound chicken lightly to about ½-inch thickness. Remove plastic wrap.

2. Place chicken in a resealable plastic bag set in a shallow dish. For marinade, combine balsamic vinegar, oil, garlic, and crushed red pepper. Pour over chicken; seal bag. Marinate in refrigerator for 4 to 24 hours, turning bag occasionally.

3. Drain chicken, discarding marinade. Sprinkle chicken with salt and black pepper. For a charcoal grill, grill chicken on the rack of an uncovered grill directly over medium coals for 8 to 11 minutes or until chicken is no longer pink (170°F), turning once halfway through grilling. (For a gas grill, preheat grill. Reduce heat to medium. Place chicken on grill rack over heat. Cover and grill as above.)

Per serving: 306 cal., 16 g total fat (2 g sat. fat), 82 mg chol., 245 mg sodium, 5 g carbo., 0 g fiber, 33 g pro.
Daily Values: 1% vit. A, 1% vit. C, 2% calcium, 7% iron

Chicken Kabobs with Thai Brushing Sauce

When making kabobs, don't cram everything together on the skewers; leaving a small space between pieces makes for more even cooking. See photo on page 88.

Prep: 15 minutes **Grill:** 10 minutes **Makes:** 4 servings

    1 small fresh pineapple (3 to 3½ pounds) (optional)
      Nonstick cooking spray (optional)
   ⅔ cup bottled sweet-and-sour sauce
    2 tablespoons snipped fresh basil
    1 teaspoon Thai seasoning or five-spice powder
    1 clove garlic, minced
    1 pound skinless, boneless chicken breast halves, cut into 1-inch pieces

1. If using pineapple, cut off the pineapple ends. Halve pineapple lengthwise; cut each half crosswise into 4 slices. Lightly coat pineapple slices with nonstick cooking spray. Set aside.

2. For sauce, in a small bowl combine sweet-and-sour sauce, basil, Thai seasoning, and garlic. Set sauce aside.

3. Thread chicken pieces onto 4 long metal skewers, leaving a ¼-inch space between pieces.

4. For a charcoal grill, grill kabobs on the rack of an uncovered grill directly over medium coals for 10 to 12 minutes or until chicken is no longer pink (170°F), turning once and brushing with ¼ cup of the sauce halfway through grilling. If using pineapple, add slices to grill rack after 5 minutes of grilling; turn once during grilling. (For a gas grill, preheat grill. Reduce heat to medium. Place kabobs and pineapple on grill rack over heat. Cover and grill as above.)

5. Reheat remaining sauce until bubbly; serve with chicken and pineapple. If desired, garnish with fresh *basil* and fresh *red chile peppers*.

Per serving: 177 cal., 2 g total fat (0 g sat. fat), 66 mg chol., 396 mg sodium, 12 g carbo., 0 g fiber, 26 g pro.
Daily Values: 3% vit. A, 2% vit. C, 3% calcium, 6% iron

Cranberry-Chipotle Drumsticks

Prep: 10 minutes **Grill:** 50 minutes **Makes:** 6 servings

- 1 16-ounce can whole cranberry sauce
- ½ cup bottled barbecue sauce
- 1 canned chipotle pepper in adobo sauce, finely chopped
- 12 chicken drumsticks

1. For sauce, combine cranberry sauce, barbecue sauce, and chipotle pepper. Reserve 1 cup of the sauce in an airtight container for dipping sauce; cover and chill. For basting sauce, transfer the remaining sauce to a blender or food processor. Cover and blend or process until smooth.

2. For a charcoal grill, arrange medium-hot coals around a drip pan. Test for medium heat above pan. Place chicken on grill rack over pan. Cover and grill for 50 to 60 minutes or until chicken is no longer pink (180°F), turning once halfway through grilling and brushing with basting sauce during the last 5 minutes of grilling. (For a gas grill, preheat grill. Reduce heat to medium. Adjust for indirect cooking. Grill as above.) Serve chicken with reserved dipping sauce.

Per serving: 368 cal., 13 g total fat (3 g sat. fat), 118 mg chol., 289 mg sodium, 32 g carbo., 1 g fiber, 29 g pro.
Daily Values: 3% vit. A, 8% vit. C, 2% calcium, 9% iron

Jalapeño Jelly-Glazed Drumsticks

This recipe is lip-smackin' proof that you don't need a smoker to cook chicken with loads of satisfying smoke flavor.

Prep: 15 minutes **Soak:** 1 hour **Grill:** 50 minutes **Makes:** 5 servings

    2 cups mesquite wood chips
  2½ to 3 pounds chicken drumsticks
    Salt and black pepper
  ½ cup jalapeño jelly

1. At least 1 hour before grilling, soak wood chips in water. If desired, remove skin from drumsticks. Sprinkle drumsticks with salt and pepper.

2. For glaze, in a small saucepan heat jalapeño jelly until melted. Set glaze aside.

3. For a charcoal grill, arrange medium-hot coals around a drip pan. Test for medium heat above pan. Drain wood chips and add to coals. Place chicken on grill rack over drip pan. Cover and grill for 50 to 60 minutes or until chicken is no longer pink (180°F), turning once halfway through grilling and brushing with glaze occasionally during the last 10 minutes of grilling. (For a gas grill, preheat grill. Reduce heat to medium. Adjust for indirect cooking. Grill as above.)

Per serving: 323 cal., 13 g total fat (4 g sat. fat), 123 mg chol., 226 mg sodium, 21 g carbo., 0 g fiber, 29 g pro.
Daily Values: 2% vit. A, 6% vit. C, 2% calcium, 8% iron

Honey-Glazed Chicken Drumsticks

Prep: 10 minutes **Grill:** 50 minutes **Makes:** 4 servings

    3 tablespoons honey

    3 tablespoons Dijon-style mustard

    1 teaspoon lemon juice

    1 teaspoon finely shredded orange peel

    8 chicken drumsticks

1. For glaze, combine honey, mustard, lemon juice, and orange peel. Set glaze aside.

2. For a charcoal grill, arrange medium-hot coals around a drip pan. Test for medium heat above pan. Place chicken on grill rack over drip pan. Cover and grill for 50 to 60 minutes or until chicken is no longer pink (180°F), turning once halfway through grilling and brushing with glaze occasionally during the last 10 minutes of grilling. (For a gas grill, preheat grill. Reduce heat to medium. Adjust for indirect cooking. Grill as above.)

Per serving: 241 cal., 9 g total fat (2 g sat. fat), 87 mg chol., 370 mg sodium, 14 g carbo., 0 g fiber, 26 g pro.
Daily Values: 1% vit. A, 2% vit. C, 1% calcium, 8% iron

Types of Thermometers

In the quest for grilled meat perfection, there's no handier tool than a good meat thermometer. Two common, useful types are the oven-/grill-safe thermometer and the instant-read thermometer.

Oven-/grill-safe thermometers are meant to remain in the food the entire time it cooks. They work best with large items such as whole poultry and roasts.

Instant-read thermometers are available in both digital and dial versions and are not designed to remain in food while it cooks. But because they can measure temperatures in just 10 to 20 seconds, they're easy to remove and reinsert as needed. This type of thermometer is particularly nice to use for thin foods, when it's necessary to insert the thermometer sideways.

For the most accurate reading, always insert any meat thermometer into the thickest part of the meat and away from any bones or fat.

Grilling Gallery

Olive-Stuffed Steaks,
page 14

BLT Steaks, page 15

Top Loins with Gorgonzola Butter, page 16

Honey-Bourbon Steaks,
page 17

Flat-Iron Steaks, page 18

Chili-Rubbed Prime Rib, page 26

Veal Rolls Stuffed with Herb Cheese, page 29

Cranberry-Chipotle Pork Chops, page 36

Lemon-and-Herb-Rubbed
Pork Chops, page 38

Stout-Glazed Ribs, page 49

Orange-Coriander-Glazed
Chicken, page **64**

Chipotle-Peach-Glazed
Chicken Thighs, page **66**

Tangy Lemon Chicken,
page 71

Chicken Kabobs with Thai Brushing Sauce, page 77

Dipping Drums, page 98

Herb-and-Lemon-Crusted
Game Hens, page 100

Maple-Cranberry Game Hens,
page 99

**Maple-Glazed Quail,
page 101**

**Turkey with
Dried Tomato Pesto,
page 104**

Stuffed Tuna Steaks, page 111

Orange Roughy with Dill, page 113

Rocky Mountain Trout, page 116

Spiced Cider Salmon,
page **120**

Planked Salmon with
Cucumber-Dill Sauce,
page **121**

Glazed Prosciutto-Wrapped Shrimp. page 125

Shrimp with Papaya Salsa, page 128

Chicken Drumsticks Extraordinaire

Jazzed-up with fresh basil and pecans, ordinary drumsticks become extraordinarily delectable.

Prep: 15 minutes **Grill:** 50 minutes **Makes:** 4 servings

    1 cup lightly packed fresh basil leaves
    ½ cup broken pecans
    ¼ cup olive oil
    2 cloves garlic, minced
    ¼ teaspoon salt
    ¼ teaspoon black pepper
    8 chicken drumsticks

1. In a blender or small food processor combine basil, pecans, oil, garlic, salt, and pepper. Cover and blend or process until almost smooth, scraping down sides as needed. Divide mixture in half; chill half of the mixture.

2. If desired, remove skin from chicken. Brush chicken with the unchilled basil mixture.

3. For a charcoal grill, arrange medium-hot coals around a drip pan. Test for medium heat above pan. Place chicken on grill rack over drip pan. Cover and grill for 50 to 60 minutes or until chicken is no longer pink (180°F), turning once halfway through grilling and brushing with the chilled basil mixture during the last 5 minutes of grilling. (For a gas grill, preheat grill. Reduce heat to medium. Adjust for indirect cooking. Grill as above.)

Per serving without skin: 453 cal., 36 g total fat (6 g sat. fat), 118 mg chol., 268 mg sodium, 3 g carbo., 2 g fiber, 30 g pro.
Daily Values: 14% vit. A, 11% vit. C, 5% calcium, 13% iron

Dipping Drums

See photo on page 89.

Prep: 15 minutes **Grill:** 50 minutes **Makes:** 4 servings

- 8 chicken drumsticks
- 3 tablespoons Worcestershire sauce for chicken
- 1 teaspoon bottled minced garlic
- ½ teaspoon poultry seasoning
- ⅛ teaspoon black pepper

    Assorted dipping sauces (such as bottled ranch salad dressing, barbecue sauce, sweet-and-sour sauce, or creamy Dijon-style mustard blend)

1. Remove skin from chicken. Combine Worcestershire sauce, garlic, poultry seasoning, and pepper; brush over chicken drumsticks.

2. For a charcoal grill, arrange medium-hot coals around a drip pan. Test for medium heat above pan. Place chicken on grill rack over drip pan. Cover and grill for 50 to 60 minutes or until chicken is tender and no longer pink (180°F), turning once halfway through grilling. (For a gas grill, preheat grill. Reduce heat to medium. Adjust for indirect cooking. Grill as above.)

3. Serve chicken with assorted dipping sauces.

Per serving: 476 cal., 31 g total fat (6 g sat. fat), 164 mg chol., 598 mg sodium, 6 g carbo., 0 g fiber, 42 g pro.
Daily Values: 2% vit. A, 2% vit. C, 4% calcium, 12% iron

Maple-Cranberry Game Hens

Brining is a must-have technique for your grilling bag of tricks. Try it with tender, juicy game hens and you can't go wrong. See photo on page 89.

Prep: 30 minutes **Marinate:** 4 hours **Grill:** 50 minutes **Stand:** 10 minutes **Makes:** 2 servings

- 2 1¼- to 1½-pound Cornish game hens
- 6 cups white cranberry juice or white grape juice
- ½ cup maple-flavored syrup
- ¼ cup coarse salt

1. Remove giblets from game hens, if present. Rinse hens. For brine, in a stainless-steel or enamel stockpot or plastic container combine cranberry juice, syrup, and salt; stir to dissolve salt.

2. Carefully add game hens to brine. Cover and marinate in the refrigerator for 4 hours, turning hens occasionally.

3. Remove game hens from brine; discard brine. Rinse hens and pat dry with paper towels. Tie drumsticks to tail with 100-percent-cotton kitchen string. Twist wing tips under back.

4. For a charcoal grill, arrange medium-hot coals around a drip pan. Test for medium heat above pan. Place the game hens, breast sides up, on grill rack over drip pan. Cover and grill for 50 to 60 minutes or until hens are no longer pink (180°F in thigh muscle). (For a gas grill, preheat grill. Reduce heat to medium. Adjust for indirect cooking. Grill as above.)

5. Remove game hens from grill. Cover with foil and let stand 10 minutes before carving. If desired, garnish with fresh *herbs*.

Per serving: 807 cal., 45 g total fat (12 g sat. fat), 346 mg chol., 1,180 mg sodium, 36 g carbo., 0 g fiber, 59 g pro.
Daily Values: 6% vit. A, 100% vit. C, 4% calcium, 14% iron

A Time to Brine

For cooking the types of lean meats, poultry, and seafood that can easily dry out on the grill, brining has lately become something of a wonder technique. Why? It's supersimple and, when done properly, can add loads of flavor and juiciness. The basic process consists of soaking meat in a mixture of salt, water, and flavorings for a set period of time. As it soaks, the meat slurps up juicy flavor that shows through deliciously in the finished dish.

But beware of too much of a good thing—soak meat for too long in brine and it grills up dry and overly salty. With brining, timing is everything, so follow recipe directions closely.

Herb-and-Lemon-Crusted Game Hens

See photo on page 89.

Prep: 30 minutes **Chill:** 12 to 24 hours **Grill:** 50 minutes **Stand:** 10 minutes **Makes:** 4 servings

      4   1¼- to 1½-pound Cornish game hens
      2   lemons
  1½   cups snipped fresh herbs (such as oregano and basil)
      2   teaspoons coarse salt or 1½ teaspoons salt
  ½   teaspoon black pepper

1. Remove giblets from game hens, if present. If desired, remove skin from hens. Rinse hens and pat dry with paper towels. Place hens on a plate or in a baking dish.

2. Finely shred enough lemon peel from 1 of the lemons to make 2 teaspoons peel. In a small bowl combine the lemon peel, herbs, salt, and pepper; set aside. Cut 1½ of the lemons into slices; cut remaining lemon half into four wedges. Place one lemon wedge into each hen cavity.

3. Tie drumsticks to tail with 100-percent-cotton kitchen string. Twist wing tips under back. Generously rub outside of game hens with herb mixture. Lay lemon slices over the top. Cover tightly with plastic wrap and refrigerate for 12 to 24 hours.

4. For a charcoal grill, arrange medium-hot coals around a drip pan. Test for medium heat above pan. Place game hens, breast sides up, on grill rack over drip pan. Cover and grill for 50 to 60 minutes or until hens are no longer pink (180°F in thigh muscle). (For a gas grill, preheat grill. Reduce heat to medium. Adjust for indirect cooking. Grill as above.)

5. Remove game hens from grill. Cover with foil and let stand 10 minutes before carving.

Per serving: 676 cal., 45 g total fat (12 g sat. fat), 346 mg chol., 1,134 mg sodium, 3 g carbo., 0 g fiber, 60 g pro.
Daily Values: 10% vit. A, 28% vit. C, 9% calcium, 14% iron

Maple-Glazed Quail

When lightly kissed by the flame, quail's delicate flavor takes flight. Be careful not to overcook these elegant birds. See photo on page 90.

Prep: 10 minutes **Chill:** 2 to 24 hours **Grill:** 15 minutes **Makes:** 8 servings

    2 teaspoons hot chili powder

    1 teaspoon dried thyme, crushed

    ¾ teaspoon salt

    8 4- to 4½-pound semiboneless quail

    ½ cup pure maple syrup

    2 tablespoons peanut oil or cooking oil

1. For rub, in a small bowl combine chili powder, thyme, and salt. Sprinkle rub evenly over quail; rub in with your fingers. Place quail in a shallow dish. Combine ¼ cup of the maple syrup and the oil; spoon over quail, turning to coat. Cover and chill for 2 to 24 hours.

2. For a charcoal grill, arrange medium-hot coals around a drip pan. Test for medium heat above pan. Place quail, breast sides down, on the greased grill rack over drip pan. Cover and grill for 15 to 20 minutes or until a meat thermometer inserted into breast portion registers 180°F, turning and brushing once halfway through grilling with the remaining ¼ cup maple syrup. (For a gas grill, preheat grill. Reduce heat to medium. Adjust for indirect cooking. Grill as above.)

3. If desired, serve with fresh *pineapple wedges* and *torn mixed salad greens*.

Per serving: 299 cal., 17 g total fat (4 g sat. fat), 86 mg chol., 275 mg sodium, 14 g carbo., 0 g fiber, 22 g pro.
Daily Values: 9% vit. A, 10% vit. C, 3% calcium, 25% iron

No-Fail Quail

A true delicacy on the grill, mild quail are surprisingly simple to prepare and serve. For the easiest grilling and eating, purchase semiboneless quail, which are sold split open with rib cages removed, and leave the wings and leg bones intact. You can purchase quail at a good butcher shop.

Turkey on the Grill

A zesty under-the-skin rub gets extra credit for taking this bird to the top of its class.

Prep: 20 minutes **Grill:** 2½ hours **Stand:** 15 minutes **Makes:** 8 to 10 servings

- 1 8- to 10-pound whole turkey
- 2 teaspoons dried Italian seasoning, basil, or oregano, crushed
- 1 teaspoon poultry seasoning
- ½ teaspoon salt
- ½ teaspoon black pepper
- 1 tablespoon cooking oil

1. Thaw turkey, if frozen. Remove neck and giblets. Rinse the turkey body cavity and pat dry with paper towels. In a small bowl combine Italian seasoning, poultry seasoning, salt, and pepper; set aside.

2. Starting at the neck on one side of the breast, slip your fingers between skin and meat, loosening the skin as you work toward the tail end. Once your entire hand is under the skin, free the skin around the top of the thigh and leg area up to, but not around, the tip of the drumstick. Repeat on the other side of the breast. Rub seasonings under the skin directly on meat. Skewer neck skin to back. Twist wing tips behind back. Tuck drumsticks under band of skin or tie to tail. If desired, insert a meat thermometer into the center of an inside thigh muscle. Brush turkey with oil.

3. For a charcoal grill, arrange medium-hot coals around a drip pan. Test for medium heat above the pan. Place turkey, breast side up, on grill rack over drip pan. Cover and grill for 2½ to 3 hours or until thermometer registers 180°F and turkey is no longer pink, adding fresh coals every 45 to 60 minutes and cutting band of skin or string the last hour of grilling. (For a gas grill, preheat grill. Reduce heat to medium. Adjust for indirect cooking. Grill as above.)

4. Remove turkey from grill. Cover with foil and let stand 15 minutes before carving.

Per serving: 723 cal., 36 g total fat (10 g sat. fat), 306 mg chol., 367 mg sodium, 0 g carbo., 0 g fiber, 93 g pro.
Daily Values: 1% vit. A, 10% calcium, 36% iron

Turkey Breast with Raspberry Salsa

Prep: 10 minutes **Grill:** 1¼ hours **Stand:** 10 minutes **Makes:** 8 servings

⅓ cup seedless raspberry jam

1 tablespoon Dijon-style mustard

1 teaspoon finely shredded orange peel

½ cup bottled mild salsa

1 2- to 2½-pound turkey breast half with bone

1. In a small bowl combine raspberry jam, mustard, and orange peel. Stir 3 tablespoons of the jam mixture into the salsa. Cover and chill both mixtures.

2. Insert a meat thermometer into the thickest part of the turkey breast half, without touching bone.

3. For a charcoal grill, arrange medium-hot coals around a drip pan. Test for medium heat above pan. Place turkey breast half, bone side down, on grill rack over drip pan. Cover and grill for 1¼ to 2 hours or until thermometer registers 170°F, brushing occasionally with reserved jam mixture during the last 15 minutes of grilling. (For a gas grill, preheat grill. Reduce heat to medium. Adjust for indirect cooking. Grill as above.)

4. Remove turkey from grill. Cover with foil and let stand 10 minutes before carving. Serve turkey with salsa mixture.

Per serving: 143 cal., 1 g total fat (0 g sat. fat), 55 mg chol., 192 mg sodium, 11 g carbo., 0 g fiber, 22 g pro.
Daily Values: 2% vit. A, 6% vit. C, 2% calcium, 6% iron

Turkey with Dried Tomato Pesto

See photo on page 90.

Prep: 15 minutes **Grill:** 1¼ hours **Stand:** 10 minutes **Makes:** 8 servings

- ⅓ cup purchased basil pesto
- 3 tablespoons chopped, drained oil-packed dried tomatoes
- 1 2- to 2½-pound turkey breast half with bone
  Salt and black pepper
- 12 ounces dried fettuccine, cooked and drained

1. In a small bowl combine pesto and dried tomatoes; set aside. Starting at the breast bone, slip your fingers between skin and meat to loosen skin, leaving skin attached at one side to make a pocket. Lift skin and spoon half of the pesto mixture evenly over turkey meat; rub in with your fingers. Fold skin back over meat, covering as much as possible. Sprinkle turkey breast half with salt and pepper. Insert a meat thermometer into the thickest part of the turkey breast without touching bone.

2. For a charcoal grill, arrange medium-hot coals around a drip pan. Test for medium heat above the pan. Place turkey breast half, bone side down, on grill rack over drip pan. Cover and grill for 1¼ to 2 hours or until thermometer registers 170°F. (For a gas grill, preheat grill. Reduce heat to medium. Adjust for indirect cooking. Grill as above.)

3. Remove turkey from grill. Cover with foil and let stand 10 minutes before carving.

4. Meanwhile, toss remaining pesto mixture with hot fettuccine. Slice turkey; serve with fettuccine. If desired, garnish with fresh *basil*.

Per serving: 328 cal., 9 g total fat (1 g sat. fat), 50 mg chol., 196 mg sodium, 34 g carbo., 1 g fiber, 26 g pro.
Daily Values: 1% vit. A, 4% vit. C, 2% calcium, 12% iron

Chili-Mustard Turkey Breast

Bone-in turkey breast is tailor-made for long, slow indirect grilling because the bone helps keep the meat from drying out too quickly.

Prep: 20 minutes **Grill:** 1¼ hours **Stand:** 10 minutes **Makes:** 8 servings

    3 tablespoons honey mustard
    1 tablespoon brown sugar
    ½ teaspoon chili powder
    ⅛ teaspoon ground cumin
    ⅛ teaspoon black pepper
    1 2- to 2½-pound turkey breast half with bone

1. For rub, combine mustard, brown sugar, chili powder, cumin, and pepper. Set rub aside.

2. Starting at the breast bone, slip your fingers between the skin and meat to loosen the skin, leaving the skin attached at the side to make a pocket. Lift the skin and spread the rub evenly over the turkey meat. Fold skin back over meat, covering as much as possible. Insert a meat thermometer into thickest part of turkey breast half without touching bone.

3. For a charcoal grill, arrange medium-hot coals around a drip pan. Test for medium heat above pan. Place turkey breast half, bone side down, on grill rack over drip pan. Cover and grill for 1¼ to 2 hours or until thermometer registers 170°F. (For a gas grill, preheat grill. Reduce heat to medium. Adjust for indirect cooking. Grill as above.)

4. Remove turkey from grill. Cover with foil and let stand 10 minutes before carving.

Per serving: 169 cal., 7 g total fat (2 g sat. fat), 66 mg chol., 81 mg sodium, 3 g carbo., 0 g fiber, 22 g pro.
Daily Values: 1% vit. A, 2% calcium, 7% iron

Easy Turkey Drumsticks

Prep: 5 minutes **Grill:** 45 minutes **Makes:** 4 servings

>   4 turkey drumsticks
>   1 tablespoon cooking oil
>   Salt and black pepper

1. Brush drumsticks with oil; sprinkle with salt and pepper.

2. For a charcoal grill, arrange medium-hot coals around a drip pan. Test for medium heat above pan. Place drumsticks on grill rack over drip pan. Cover and grill for 45 minutes to 1¼ hours or until turkey is no longer pink (180°F), turning occasionally. (For a gas grill, preheat grill. Reduce heat to medium. Adjust for indirect cooking. Grill as above.)

Per serving: 424 cal., 17 g total fat (5 g sat. fat), 274 mg chol., 448 mg sodium, 0 g carbo., 0 g fiber, 64 g pro.
Daily Values: 6% calcium, 28% iron

Food Safety at the Grill

The very best way to prevent foodborne illness when grilling is to cook meat to a minimum internal temperature, as directed in the recipes. Also practice the following:

- Keep raw foods separate from cooked foods.

- Wash your hands and cutting boards frequently.

- Don't use the same plates or utensils for raw and cooked foods.

- Don't reuse leftover marinades or brush-ons unless they are brought to a full and vigorous boil for at least one minute before use.

- Keep hot foods hot and cold foods cold. Don't let any cooked food sit out at room temperature for more than two hours.

fish & seafood

Lemon-Dill Fish Fillets

Prep: 15 minutes **Grill:** 12 minutes **Makes:** 4 servings

- 1 pound fresh or frozen fish fillets, ½ to ¾ inch thick
- 1 lemon, thinly sliced
- 2 tablespoons snipped fresh dill or 1 teaspoon dried dill
- ½ teaspoon lemon-pepper seasoning
- 1 tablespoon drained capers

1. Thaw fish, if frozen. Rinse fish; pat dry with paper towels. Cut fish into 4 serving-size pieces, if necessary.

2. Tear off four 24×18-inch pieces of heavy foil; fold each in half to make 12×18-inch rectangles. Arrange lemon slices in the center of each foil rectangle. Top each with a fish fillet, tucking under any thin edges. Sprinkle fish evenly with dill, lemon-pepper seasoning, and capers. Bring up two opposite edges of foil and seal with a double fold. Fold the remaining edges together to completely enclose mixture, leaving space for steam to build.

3. For a charcoal grill, grill foil packets on the rack of an uncovered grill directly over medium coals for 12 to 18 minutes or until fish flakes easily when tested with a fork (carefully open one packet to check for doneness), turning packet once. (For a gas grill, preheat grill. Reduce heat to medium. Place foil packets on grill rack over heat. Cover and grill as above.)

Per serving: 97 cal., 1 g total fat (0 g sat. fat), 48 mg chol., 261 mg sodium, 2 g carbo., 0 g fiber, 20 g pro.
Daily Values: 1% vit. A, 13% vit. C, 2% calcium, 3% iron

Red Snapper and Vegetables

Convenient cleanup and wicked-good flavor make foil packet grilling the go-to technique for succulent fish hot off the grill.

Prep: 20 minutes **Cook:** 5 minutes **Grill:** 20 minutes **Makes:** 4 servings

  4 6-ounces fresh or frozen red snapper fillets (with skin), ½ to ¾ inch thick

12 ounces whole tiny new potatoes, Yukon gold potatoes, or purple potatoes, quartered

  2 cups broccoli florets

 ⅓ cup purchased basil pesto

1. Thaw fish, if frozen. Rinse fish and pat dry with paper towels. If desired, remove and discard skin; set fish aside.

2. Place potatoes in a medium microwave-safe bowl. Microwave, covered, on 100 percent power (high) for 5 to 7 minutes or until nearly tender, stirring once. Add broccoli and half of the pesto; toss to coat.

3. Tear off four 12-inch squares of heavy foil. Divide vegetable mixture into 4 portions; place 1 portion in the center of each foil square. Top each with a fish fillet, tucking under any thin edges. Spoon remaining pesto over fish. Bring up two opposite edges of foil and seal with a double fold. Fold remaining edges together to enclose mixture, leaving space for steam to build.

4. For a charcoal grill, grill foil packets on the rack of an uncovered grill directly over medium coals for 20 to 25 minutes or until fish flakes easily when tested with a fork (carefully open one packet to check for doneness), turning packet once. (For a gas grill, preheat grill. Reduce heat to medium. Place packets on grill rack over heat. Cover and grill as above.) If desired, serve with additional purchased basil pesto.

Per serving: 375 cal., 16 g total fat (0 g sat. fat), 45 mg chol., 174 mg sodium, 21 g carbo., 3 g fiber, 40 g pro.
Daily Values: 6% vit. A, 78% vit. C, 6% calcium, 14% iron

Mustard-Glazed Halibut Steaks

Prep: 10 minutes **Grill:** 8 minutes **Makes:** 4 servings

- 4 6-ounce fresh or frozen halibut steaks, 1 inch thick
- 2 tablespoons butter or margarine
- 2 tablespoons lemon juice
- 1 tablespoon Dijon-style mustard
- 2 teaspoons snipped fresh basil or ½ teaspoon dried basil, crushed

1. Thaw fish, if frozen. Rinse fish; pat dry with paper towels. In a small saucepan heat butter, lemon juice, mustard, and basil over low heat until melted. Brush both sides of fish with mustard mixture.

2. For a charcoal grill, grill fish on the greased rack of an uncovered grill directly over medium coals for 8 to 12 minutes or until fish flakes easily when tested with a fork, gently turning once and brushing occasionally with mustard mixture halfway through grilling. (For a gas grill, preheat grill. Reduce heat to medium. Place fish on greased grill rack over heat. Cover and grill as above.)

Per serving: 243 cal., 10 g total fat (4 g sat. fat), 69 mg chol., 223 mg sodium, 1 g carbo., 0 g fiber, 36 g pro.
Daily Values: 9% vit. A, 6% vit. C, 9% calcium, 9% iron

Stuffed Tuna Steaks

Meaty tuna is one of the easiest fish to grill. A piquant olive, onion, and sweet pepper stuffing lends extra pizzazz to every bite. See photo on page 91.

Prep: 25 minutes **Grill:** 8 minutes **Makes:** 6 servings

    6 6-ounce fresh or frozen tuna steaks, 1 inch thick
    ¼ cup finely chopped onion
    ¼ cup pimiento-stuffed green olives, finely chopped
    ¼ cup finely chopped red sweet pepper
    1 tablespoon hot chile oil

1. Thaw fish, if frozen. Rinse fish; pat dry with paper towels. For stuffing, combine onion, olives, and sweet pepper.

2. Cut a horizontal pocket in each tuna steak by cutting from one side to, but not through, the other side. Spoon about 2 tablespoons of the stuffing into each pocket. If necessary, secure the pocket shut with short metal skewers or wooden toothpicks. Brush half of the hot chile oil over both sides of the tuna steaks.

3. For a charcoal grill, grill fish on the greased rack of an uncovered grill directly over medium coals for 8 to 12 minutes or until fish flakes easily when tested with a fork, gently turning and brushing once with the remaining hot chile oil halfway through grilling. (For a gas grill, preheat grill. Reduce heat to medium. Place fish on greased grill rack over heat. Cover and grill as above.)

Per serving: 279 cal., 12 g total fat (2 g sat. fat), 64 mg chol., 149 mg sodium, 1 g carbo., 0 g fiber, 40 g pro.
Daily Values: 72% vit. A, 22% vit. C, 2% calcium, 10% iron

Dijon Tuna Steaks

Prep: 20 minutes **Grill:** 8 minutes **Makes:** 4 servings

    4 6-ounce fresh or frozen tuna or halibut steaks, 1 inch thick
       Salt
    2 teaspoons cooking oil
       Dash cayenne pepper
    1 tablespoon Dijon-style mustard
    1 recipe Jalapeño Mayo (page 183) (optional)

1. Thaw fish, if frozen. Rinse fish and pat dry with paper towels. Sprinkle fish with salt. In a small bowl combine oil and cayenne pepper; brush over both sides of fish.

2. For a charcoal grill, grill fish on the greased rack of an uncovered grill directly over medium coals for 8 to 12 minutes or until fish flakes easily when tested with a fork, gently turning and brushing with mustard halfway through grilling. (For a gas grill, preheat grill. Reduce heat to medium. Place fish on greased grill rack over heat. Cover and grill as above.) If desired, serve fish with Jalapeño Mayo.

Per serving: 208 cal., 4 g total fat (1 g sat. fat), 77 mg chol., 298 mg sodium, 1 g carbo., 0 g fiber, 41 g pro.
Daily Values: 2% vit. A, 3% vit. C, 3% calcium, 7% iron

Orange Roughy with Dill

Orange slices do double duty, adding zesty flavor as well as creating a slick platform on which to grill the fish. See photo on page 92.

Prep: 15 minutes **Grill:** 6 minutes **Makes:** 4 servings

- 4 5- to 6-ounce fresh or frozen orange roughy or sea bass fillets, ¾ inch thick
- 2 tablespoons olive oil
- 2 tablespoons snipped fresh dill
- ¼ teaspoon salt
- ¼ teaspoon white pepper
- 5 large oranges

1. Thaw fish, if frozen. Rinse fish and pat dry with paper towels. Combine oil, dill, salt, and white pepper. Brush dill mixture over both sides of fish.

2. Cut 4 of the oranges into ¼-inch slices. For a charcoal grill, arrange a bed of orange slices on a greased grill rack. Arrange the fish on the orange slices. Grill orange slices and fish on the rack of an uncovered grill directly over medium coals for 6 to 9 minutes or until fish flakes easily when tested with a fork. (For a gas grill, preheat grill. Reduce heat to medium. Arrange orange slices and fish on greased grill rack over heat. Cover and grill as above.)

3. To serve, use a spatula to transfer the sea bass and grilled orange slices to a serving platter. Cut the remaining orange into wedges; squeeze juice from wedges over fish.

Per serving: 268 cal., 10 g total fat (2 g sat. fat), 58 mg chol., 242 mg sodium, 18 g carbo., 3 g fiber, 28 g pro.
Daily Values: 11% vit. A, 133% vit. C, 7% calcium, 4% iron

Swordfish with Cucumber-Mint Sauce

A variation on classic Greek tzatziki, this tangy, refreshing cucumber sauce is the perfect foil for mellow and satisfying swordfish.

Prep: 10 minutes **Grill:** 8 minutes **Makes:** 4 servings

- 1 to 1¼ pounds fresh or frozen swordfish or halibut steaks, 1 inch thick
- ⅓ cup plain low-fat yogurt
- ¼ cup finely chopped cucumber
- 1 teaspoon snipped fresh mint or ¼ teaspoon dried mint, crushed
- Dash black pepper

1. Thaw fish, if frozen. Rinse fish and pat dry with paper towels. Cut fish into 4 serving-size pieces, if necessary.

2. For sauce, in a small bowl combine yogurt, cucumber, mint, and pepper. Cover and chill until serving time.

3. For a charcoal grill, grill fish on the greased grill rack of an uncovered grill directly over medium coals for 8 to 12 minutes or until fish flakes easily when tested with a fork, gently turning once halfway through grilling. (For a gas grill, preheat grill. Reduce heat to medium. Place fish on greased grill rack over heat. Cover and grill as above.)

4. Serve swordfish with sauce.

Per serving: 148 cal., 5 g total fat (1 g sat. fat), 44 mg chol., 117 mg sodium, 2 g carbo., 0 g fiber, 24 g pro.
Daily Values: 3% vit. A, 3% vit. C, 4% calcium, 6% iron

Cilantro-Lime Trout

Prep: 15 minutes **Grill:** 8 minutes **Makes:** 4 servings

   4 8- to 10-ounce fresh or frozen dressed trout, heads removed

   3 tablespoons lime juice

   2 tablespoons olive oil

   2 tablespoons snipped fresh cilantro or parsley

  ½ teaspoon salt

  ¼ teaspoon cracked black pepper

      Lime wedges (optional)

1. Thaw trout, if frozen. Rinse trout and pat dry with paper towels. In a small bowl combine lime juice and oil. Brush the inside and outside of each trout with juice mixture. Sprinkle cilantro, salt, and pepper evenly inside the cavity of each fish.

2. Place trout in a well-greased grill basket. For a charcoal grill, place basket on the rack of an uncovered grill directly over medium coals. Grill for 8 to 12 minutes or until trout flakes easily when tested with a fork, turning basket once halfway through grilling. (For a gas grill, preheat grill. Reduce heat to medium. Place trout in a well-greased grill basket. Place grill basket on grill rack over heat. Cover and grill as above.) If desired, serve trout with lime wedges.

Per serving: 259 cal., 14 g total fat (3 g sat. fat), 83 mg chol., 342 mg sodium, 1 g carbo., 0 g fiber, 30 g pro.
Daily Values: 10% vit. A, 13% vit. C, 10% calcium, 3% iron

Rocky Mountain Trout

If you're fishing for compliments, this recipe will land you a bounty. It works well on camp stoves and campfires too. See photo on page 93.

Prep: 15 minutes **Grill:** 8 minutes **Makes:** 4 servings

 4 8- to 10-ounce fresh or frozen pan-dressed rainbow trout
    Cooking oil
 ½ to ¾ cup finely chopped red onion and/or green sweet pepper
 2 tablespoons snipped fresh cilantro
 ½ teaspoon ground cumin
 ¼ teaspoon salt
 ¼ teaspoon black pepper
    Grilled lemon wedges (optional)

1. Thaw trout, if frozen. Rinse trout and pat dry with paper towels. Brush the outside of each trout with a little bit of oil. Combine onion, cilantro, cumin, salt, and pepper. Spoon some of the onion mixture inside each trout cavity.

2. Place trout in a well-greased grill basket. For a charcoal grill, place basket on the rack of an uncovered grill directly over medium coals. Grill for 8 to 12 minutes or until trout flakes easily when tested with a fork, turning basket once halfway through grilling. (For a gas grill, preheat grill. Reduce heat to medium. Place trout in a well-greased grill basket. Place grill basket on grill rack over heat. Cover and grill as above.) If desired, serve trout with lemon wedges.

Per serving: 340 cal., 15 g total fat (4 g sat. fat), 133 mg chol., 228 mg sodium, 2 g carbo., 0 g fiber, 48 g pro.
Daily Values: 14% vit. A, 22% vit. C, 16% calcium, 5% iron

Dilly Salmon Fillets

Prep: 15 minutes **Marinate:** 10 minutes
Grill: 7 minutes per ½-inch thickness **Makes:** 4 servings

4 6-ounce fresh or frozen skinless salmon fillets, ½ to ¾ inch thick

3 tablespoons lemon juice

2 tablespoons snipped fresh dill

2 tablespoons mayonnaise or salad dressing

2 teaspoons Dijon-style mustard

Dash black pepper

1. Thaw fish, if frozen. Rinse fish and pat dry with paper towels. Place fish in a shallow dish. In a small bowl combine lemon juice and 1 tablespoon of the dill; pour over fish. Marinate at room temperature for 10 minutes. Meanwhile, in a small bowl combine the remaining 1 tablespoon dill, mayonnaise, mustard, and pepper; set aside.

2. For a charcoal grill, arrange medium-hot coals around a drip pan. Test for medium heat above the pan. Place fish on the greased grill rack over drip pan, tucking under any thin edges. Cover and grill for 7 to 9 minutes per ½-inch thickness or until fish flakes easily when tested with a fork, gently turning once and spreading with the mayonnaise mixture halfway through grilling. (For a gas grill, preheat grill. Reduce heat to medium. Adjust for indirect cooking. Cover and grill as above.)

Per serving: 211 cal., 11 g total fat (2 g sat. fat), 35 mg chol., 204 mg sodium, 1 g carbo., 0 g fiber, 25 g pro.
Daily Values: 4% vit. A, 8% vit. C, 1% calcium, 7% iron

Wild Salmon

The sumptuous flavor and texture of wild Pacific salmon is worth waiting for all year. Conveniently, wild salmon season coincides perfectly with peak grilling season—from spring through fall. Richest in flavor, Chinook or king salmon is among the most prized of all, followed by sockeye or red salmon, and coho, also known as silver salmon. All three make great choices for the grill.

Teriyaki-Glazed Salmon

Prep: 15 minutes **Cook:** 5 minutes **Grill:** 4 minutes per ½-inch thickness **Makes:** 4 servings

4 6-ounce fresh or frozen skinless salmon fillets, ½ to 1 inch thick
½ cup balsamic vinegar
1 tablespoon brown sugar or full-flavored molasses
1 teaspoon soy sauce
⅛ teaspoon ground ginger

1. Thaw fish, if frozen. Rinse fish and pat dry with paper towels. For glaze, in a small saucepan bring vinegar to boiling over medium heat. Boil gently, uncovered, about 5 minutes or until reduced by about half. Stir in the brown sugar, soy sauce, and ginger. Brush both sides of salmon with glaze.

2. For a charcoal grill, grill salmon on the greased grill rack of an uncovered grill directly over medium coals for 4 to 6 minutes per ½-inch thickness or until salmon flakes easily when tested with a fork, turning once and brushing with glaze halfway through grilling. (For a gas grill, preheat grill. Reduce heat to medium. Place salmon on grill rack over heat. Cover and grill as above.)

Per serving: 366 cal., 18 g total fat (4 g sat. fat), 99 mg chol., 184 mg sodium, 12 g carbo., 0 g fiber, 34 g pro.
Daily Values: 2% vit. A, 9% vit. C, 3% calcium, 5% iron

Spicy Grilled Salmon

This particular combination of spices kicks up the flavor in a massive way.

Prep: 15 minutes **Grill:** 4 minutes per ½-inch thickness **Makes:** 4 servings

1 1-pound fresh or frozen salmon fillet (with skin), ¾ to 1 inch thick
2 teaspoons ground coriander
2 teaspoons ground cumin
½ teaspoon salt
¼ teaspoon cayenne pepper

1. Thaw fish, if frozen. Rinse fish and pat dry with paper towels.

2. For rub, in a small bowl combine coriander, cumin, salt, and cayenne pepper. Sprinkle rub evenly over both sides of salmon; rub in with your fingers.

3. For a charcoal grill, grill salmon, skin side up, on the greased rack of a uncovered grill directly over medium coals for 4 to 6 minutes per ½-inch thickness or until fish flakes easily when tested with a fork. (For a gas grill, preheat grill. Reduce heat to medium. Place salmon on greased grill rack over heat. Cover and grill as above.)

Per serving: 218 cal., 13 g total fat (2 g sat. fat), 66 mg chol., 360 mg sodium, 2 g carbo., 1 g fiber, 23 g pro.
Daily Values: 2% vit. A, 10% vit. C, 3% calcium, 5% iron

Spiced Cider Salmon

This salty-sweet brine features allspice for exotic flavor and moist delectability. See photo on page 94.

Prep: 10 minutes **Marinate:** 2 to 3 hours **Grill:** 10 minutes **Makes:** 6 servings

    1 1½-pound fresh or frozen skinless salmon fillet, ¾ inch thick
    4 cups apple cider or apple juice
    3 tablespoons coarse salt
    2 tablespoons brown sugar
    1 teaspoon ground allspice
       Nonstick cooking spray
    2 tablespoons apple jelly (optional)

1. Thaw fish, if frozen. For brine, in a large bowl combine apple cider, salt, brown sugar, and allspice. Stir until salt and brown sugar dissolve. Add salmon. Cover and chill for 2 to 3 hours, turning salmon occasionally.

2. Drain salmon, discarding brine. Rinse salmon and pat dry with paper towels. Cut salmon into 6 serving-size pieces. Tear off a 28×12-inch piece of heavy foil; fold in half to make a 14×12-inch rectangle. Cut several slits in the foil rectangle. Lightly coat one side of the foil with cooking spray. Place salmon on the coated side of the foil.

3. For a charcoal grill, arrange medium-hot coals around a drip pan. Test for medium heat above pan. Place salmon on foil over drip pan. Cover and grill about 10 minutes or until salmon flakes easily when tested with a fork. (For a gas grill, preheat grill. Reduce heat to medium. Adjust for indirect cooking. Cover and grill as above.) If desired, brush with melted apple jelly during the last 2 minutes of grilling.

Per serving: 223 cal., 12 g total fat (2 g sat. fat), 66 mg chol., 550 mg sodium, 4 g carbo., 0 g fiber, 23 g pro.
Daily Values: 1% vit. A, 6% vit. C, 2% calcium, 3% iron

Planked Salmon with Cucumber-Dill Sauce

See photo on page 94.

Prep: 10 minutes **Chill:** 8 to 24 hours **Soak:** 1 hour
Grill: 18 minutes **Makes:** 4 to 6 servings

- 1 1½-pound fresh or frozen salmon fillet (with skin), 1 inch thick
- 1 tablespoon brown sugar
- 1 teaspoon salt
- ¼ teaspoon black pepper
- 1 12×6×¾-inch cedar grill plank
- 1 recipe Cucumber-Dill Sauce (page 158) (optional)

1. Thaw salmon, if frozen. Rinse salmon and pat dry with paper towels. Place salmon, skin side down, in a shallow dish. For rub, in a small bowl combine brown sugar, salt, and pepper. Sprinkle rub evenly over salmon (not on skin side); rub in with your fingers. Cover and chill for 8 to 24 hours.

2. At least 1 hour before grilling, soak plank in enough water to cover, weighting it to keep it submerged.

3. For a charcoal grill, arrange medium-hot coals around edge of grill. Test for medium heat in center of grill. Place salmon, skin side down, on plank. Place plank in center of grill rack. Cover and grill for 18 to 22 minutes or until salmon flakes easily when tested with a fork. (For a gas grill, preheat grill. Reduce heat to medium. Adjust heat for indirect cooking. Grill as above.)

4. To serve, cut salmon into four or six pieces. Slide a spatula between the fish and skin to release pieces from plank. If desired, serve with Cucumber-Dill Sauce, fresh *dill, lemon slices*, and/or *cucumber slices*.

Per serving: 314 cal., 17 g total fat (4 g sat. fat), 96 mg chol., 757 mg sodium, 5 g carbo., 0 g fiber, 35 g pro.
Daily Values: 2% vit. A, 2% vit. C, 8% calcium, 8% iron

Salmon with Lemon Thyme

Prep: 10 minutes **Soak:** 1 hour **Grill:** 20 minutes **Makes:** 14 servings

    2 12×6×¾-inch cedar grill planks
    2 2-pound fresh or frozen salmon fillets (with skin), 1 inch thick
    3 tablespoons olive oil
    2 teaspoons snipped fresh lemon thyme
    ½ teaspoon salt
    ½ teaspoon black pepper
    1 lemon

1. At least 1 hour before grilling, soak planks in enough water to cover, weighting them to keep them submerged. Thaw salmon, if frozen. Rinse salmon; pat dry with paper towels.

2. Place one salmon fillet on each plank, skin side down. Brush some of the olive oil over each fillet, making sure the top side is coated. Sprinkle each fillet with lemon thyme, salt, and pepper.

3. For a charcoal grill, place plank on grill rack directly over low coals. Cover and grill about 20 minutes or until salmon flakes easily when tested with a fork. (For a gas grill, preheat grill. Reduce heat to low. Place planks on grill rack over heat. Cover and grill as above.)

4. Just before serving, cut lemon into quarters; squeeze juice over salmon.

Per serving: 263 cal., 17 g total fat (3 g sat. fat), 76 mg chol., 160 mg sodium, 0 g carbo., 0 g fiber, 26 g pro.
Daily Values: 1% vit. A, 10% vit. C, 2% calcium, 3% iron

Grilling with Planks

Grilling planks add distinctive flavor to many types of meat, fish, and poultry. Most cookware stores stock planks, as well as specialty sites on the Internet. In addition to popular Western red cedar planks, maple, oak, and alder planks are all worth a try. Experiment with several types of wood to find the flavor you prefer.

Before grilling, soak planks in water for a minimum of one hour. And while grilling, keep a spray bottle handy because planks can catch on fire if they get too hot.

Orange-Marinated Salmon Steaks

Prep: 10 minutes **Marinate:** 1 to 2 hours **Grill:** 8 minutes **Makes:** 4 servings

    4 fresh or frozen salmon steaks, 1 inch thick
    ½ cup orange juice
    3 tablespoons olive oil
    ¼ teaspoon lemon-pepper seasoning

1. Thaw fish, if frozen. Rinse fish and pat dry with paper towels. Place fish in a resealable plastic bag set in a shallow dish.

2. For marinade, combine orange juice and olive oil. Pour over fish; seal bag. Marinate in refrigerator for 1 to 2 hours, turning bag occasionally.

3. Drain fish, discarding marinade. Sprinkle both sides of fish with lemon-pepper seasoning. For a charcoal grill, grill fish on the greased rack of an uncovered grill directly over medium coals for 8 to 12 minutes or until fish flakes easily when tested with a fork, gently turning once halfway through grilling. (For a gas grill, preheat grill. Reduce heat to medium. Place fish on greased grill rack over heat. Cover and grill as above.)

Per serving: 284 cal., 18 g total fat (3 g sat. fat), 83 mg chol., 152 mg sodium, 1 g carbo., 0 g fiber, 28 g pro.
Daily Values: 2% vit. A, 14% vit. C, 2% calcium, 3% iron

Foil-Wrapped Salmon Dinner

With an entrée and two sides all wrapped up and ready to serve, you can use your extra time to make an indulgent grilled dessert.

Prep: 20 minutes **Grill:** 12 minutes **Makes:** 4 servings

  4 fresh or frozen skinless salmon fillets, ½ to ¾ inch thick
     Nonstick cooking spray
  1 20-ounce package refrigerated sliced potatoes
  6 tablespoons butter or margarine, cut into 12 equal pieces
  2 teaspoons lemon-pepper seasoning
  1 pound fresh asparagus spears, trimmed

1. Thaw fish, if frozen. Rinse fish and pat dry with paper towels.

2. Tear off four 18-inch squares of heavy foil. Lightly coat one side of each piece of foil with cooking spray. On each piece of foil, place one-fourth of the sliced potatoes in two 6-inch strips, side by side in the center of the foil; top with 2 pieces of butter. Sprinkle with ¼ teaspoon of the lemon-pepper seasoning. Top with 1 salmon steak, one-fourth of the asparagus, another piece of butter, and ¼ teaspoon lemon-pepper seasoning.

3. Bring up two opposite edges of foil and seal with a double fold. Fold remaining edges together to completely enclose fish and vegetables, leaving space for steam to build.

4. For a charcoal grill, grill foil packets, potato sides down, on the rack of an uncovered grill directly over medium coals for 12 to 14 minutes or until fish flakes easily when tested with a fork and potatoes are heated through (carefully open one packet to check doneness). (For a gas grill, preheat grill. Reduce heat to medium. Place foil packets on grill rack over heat. Cover and grill as above.)

Per serving: 506 cal., 25 g total fat (12 g sat. fat), 137 mg chol., 804 mg sodium, 30 g carbo., 2 g fiber, 39 g pro.
Daily Values: 19% vit. A, 41% vit. C, 4% calcium, 13% iron

Glazed Prosciutto-Wrapped Shrimp

These prosciutto-wrapped beauties will be scarfed within seconds of leaving your grill. Better be ready with reinforcements! See photo on page 95.

Prep: 30 minutes **Grill:** 6 minutes **Makes:** 4 servings

    24 fresh or frozen large shrimp in shells
    ½ cup bourbon grilling sauce (such as Jack Daniel's)
    ½ teaspoon chili powder
     8 thin slices prosciutto

1. Thaw shrimp, if frozen. Peel and devein shrimp. Rinse shrimp and pat dry with paper towels. Set shrimp aside.

2. For sauce, in a small bowl combine grilling sauce and chili powder. Cut each prosciutto slice lengthwise into three strips. Wrap one prosciutto strip around each shrimp. Thread shrimp onto four long metal skewers, leaving a ¼-inch space between each piece. Brush shrimp with sauce.

3. For a charcoal grill, grill shrimp on the rack of an uncovered grill directly over medium coals for 6 to 9 minutes or until shrimp are opaque, turning once halfway through grilling and brushing occasionally with sauce. (For a gas grill, preheat grill. Reduce heat to medium. Place shrimp on grill rack over heat. Cover and grill as above.) If desired, serve with hot cooked *couscous*.

Per serving: 195 cal., 4 g total fat (1 g sat. fat), 207 mg chol., 932 mg sodium, 5 g carbo., 0 g fiber, 32 g pro.
Daily Values: 12% vit. A, 7% vit. C, 7% calcium, 18% iron

Cilantro Shrimp

Don't settle for shrimpy shrimp; go for the big boys this time around. Hit 'em early and often with the killer brush-on sauce.

Prep: 20 minutes **Grill:** 7 minutes **Makes:** 4 servings

- 1 pound fresh or frozen jumbo shrimp in shells (about 20)
- 2 tablespoons snipped fresh cilantro
- 1 tablespoon lemon juice
- 1 tablespoon melted butter
- 1½ to 2 teaspoons bottled minced garlic
- 1 fresh red serrano chile pepper, seeded and finely chopped (optional) (see tip, page 34)

1. Thaw shrimp, if frozen. With a sharp paring knife, split each shrimp down the back through the shell, leaving the tails intact; devein shrimp. Flatten shrimp with your hand or the flat side of a knife blade. Rinse shrimp and pat dry with paper towels.

2. For sauce, combine cilantro, lemon juice, butter, garlic, and, if desired, serrano pepper. Place shrimp, split sides down, in a lightly greased grill basket. Brush shrimp with sauce.

3. For a charcoal grill, grill shrimp on the rack of an uncovered grill directly over medium coals for 7 to 9 minutes or until shrimp are opaque, turning basket once halfway through grilling. (For a gas grill, preheat grill. Reduce heat to medium. Place shrimp in basket on grill rack over heat. Cover and grill as above.)

Per serving: 120 cal., 4 g total fat (2 g sat. fat), 137 mg chol., 148 mg sodium, 2 g carbo., 0 g fiber, 18 g pro.
Daily Values: 8% vit. A, 8% vit. C, 5% calcium, 12% iron

Garlic-Buttered Shrimp Kabobs

Prep: 30 minutes **Grill:** 7 minutes **Makes:** 4 servings

- 1 **pound fresh or frozen jumbo shrimp in shells (about 20)**
- 2 **tablespoons butter**
- 1 **tablespoon snipped fresh parsley (optional)**
- 1 **teaspoon bottled minced garlic**
  Dash cayenne pepper
- 3 **tablespoons dry white wine**

1. Thaw shrimp, if frozen. Peel and devein shrimp, leaving tails intact. Rinse shrimp and pat dry with paper towels. Thread shrimp onto four long or eight short metal skewers, leaving a ¼-inch space between each shrimp.

2. For sauce, in a small saucepan melt butter over medium heat. Stir in parsley (if desired), garlic, and cayenne pepper. Cook for 1 minute. Stir in wine; heat through. Set sauce aside.

3. For a charcoal grill, grill kabobs on the greased rack of uncovered grill directly over medium coals for 7 to 9 minutes or until shrimp are opaque, turning once halfway through grilling and brushing often with sauce. (For a gas grill, preheat grill. Reduce heat to medium. Place kabobs on grill rack over heat. Cover and grill as above.)

Per serving: 152 cal., 7 g total fat (4 g sat. fat), 145 mg chol., 167 mg sodium, 2 g carbo., 0 g fiber, 17 g pro.
Daily Values: 7% vit. A, 3% vit. C, 5% calcium, 10% iron

Shrimp with Papaya Salsa

See photo on page 96.

Prep: 15 minutes **Grill:** 6 minutes **Makes:** 6 servings

1½ pounds fresh or frozen large shrimp in shells

  1 tablespoon butter or margarine, melted

  ¼ teaspoon salt

  ¼ teaspoon ground cumin

  ¼ teaspoon black pepper

  ⅛ teaspoon cayenne pepper

  1 recipe Papaya Salsa (page 185)

1. Thaw shrimp, if frozen. Peel and devein shrimp, leaving tails intact. Rinse shrimp and pat dry with paper towels. In a small bowl combine butter, salt, cumin, black pepper, and cayenne pepper. Drizzle over shrimp, tossing to coat.

2. Place shrimp in a lightly greased grill basket. For a charcoal grill, grill shrimp on the rack of an uncovered grill directly over medium coals for 6 to 9 minutes or until shrimp are opaque, turning basket once halfway through grilling. (For a gas grill, preheat grill. Reduce heat to medium. Place shrimp in basket on grill rack over heat. Cover and grill as above.) Serve shrimp with Papaya Salsa and, if desired, grilled *pineapple wedges.*

Per serving: 102 cal., 3 g total fat (1 g sat. fat), 136 mg chol., 259 mg sodium, 5 g carbo., 0 g fiber, 14 g pro.
Daily Values: 19% vit. A, 56% vit. C, 15% iron

Thai-Spiced Scallop Kabobs

Giant-size sea scallops take to the grill like nobody's business. Consider double-skewering these for a little extra security over the flame.

Prep: 10 minutes **Grill:** 5 minutes **Makes:** 4 servings

- 1 pound fresh or frozen sea scallops
- ⅔ cup bottled sweet-and-sour sauce
- 2 tablespoons snipped fresh basil
- 1 teaspoon Thai seasoning or five-spice powder
- ½ teaspoon bottled minced garlic

1. Thaw scallops, if frozen. Rinse scallops and pat dry with paper towels. For sauce, in a small bowl combine sweet-and-sour sauce, basil, Thai seasoning, and garlic. Set aside ¼ cup of the sauce to use for basting. Reserve remaining sauce until ready to serve.

2. Thread scallops onto four 8- to 10-inch-long metal skewers, leaving a ¼-inch space between each scallop.

3. For a charcoal grill, grill kabobs on the greased rack of an uncovered grill directly over medium coals for 5 to 8 minutes or until scallops are opaque, turning once halfway through grilling and brushing once with the basting sauce. (For a charcoal grill, preheat grill. Reduce heat to medium. Place kabobs on grill rack over heat. Cover and grill as above.) Serve scallops with reserved sauce.

Per serving: 148 cal., 1 g total fat (0 g sat. fat), 37 mg chol., 517 mg sodium, 15 g carbo., 0 g fiber, 19 g pro.
Daily Values: 4% vit. A, 7% vit. C, 4% calcium, 3% iron

Lobster Tails with Chive Butter

Whether you're a seasoned captain of the coals or a wet-behind-the-wood-chips rookie, lobster on the grill is one dish that'll never let you down.

Prep: 10 minutes **Grill:** 11 minutes **Makes:** 4 servings

4 6-ounce fresh or frozen rock lobster tails

⅓ cup butter

2 tablespoons snipped fresh chives

1 teaspoon finely shredded lemon peel

Lemon wedges (optional)

1. Thaw lobster tails, if frozen. Rinse lobster and pat dry with paper towels. Using kitchen shears or a large sharp knife, butterfly each lobster tail by cutting through the center of the hard top shells and meat. Spread the tail halves apart.

2. For sauce, melt butter in a small saucepan. Remove saucepan from heat; stir in chives and lemon peel. Remove 2 tablespoons of the sauce for basting; set remaining sauce aside for dipping.

3. Brush lobster meat with some of the 2 tablespoons sauce. For a charcoal grill, grill lobster tails, cut sides down, on the rack of an uncovered grill directly over medium coals for 11 to 14 minutes or until meat is opaque in center, turning once and brushing with the remaining 2 tablespoons sauce halfway through grilling. Do not overcook. (For a gas grill, preheat grill. Reduce heat to medium. Place lobster tails on grill rack over heat. Cover and grill as above.)

4. Meanwhile, heat the reserved dipping sauce, stirring occasionally. Transfer sauce to small bowls; serve with lobster. If desired, serve with lemon wedges.

Per serving: 214 cal., 17 g total fat (10 g sat. fat), 118 mg chol., 395 mg sodium, 1 g carbo., 0 g fiber, 15 g pro.
Daily Values: 17% vit. A, 3% vit. C, 4% calcium, 1% iron

burgers &
sandwiches

Beer and Pretzel Burgers

Prep: 20 minutes **Grill:** 14 minutes **Makes:** 8 servings

⅔ cup beer or tomato juice

½ cup crushed pretzels

2 to 4 tablespoons finely chopped onion

2 tablespoons pickle relish (optional)

½ teaspoon salt

2½ pounds lean ground beef

8 hamburger buns, split and toasted

1. In a large bowl combine beer, pretzels, onion, relish (if desired), and salt. Add ground beef; mix well. Shape beef mixture into eight ¾-inch-thick patties.

2. For a charcoal grill, grill burgers on the rack of an uncovered grill directly over medium coals for 14 to 18 minutes or until done (160°F), turning once halfway through grilling. (For a gas grill, preheat grill. Reduce heat to medium. Place burgers on grill rack over heat. Cover and grill as above.) Serve burgers on buns.

Per serving: 379 cal., 15 g total fat (6 g sat. fat), 89 mg chol., 21 mg sodium, 26 g carbo., 1 g fiber, 30 g pro.
Daily Values: 7% calcium, 23% iron

Burger Doneness

Don't rely on the meat's color to gauge whether a burger is completely cooked—the color of ground beef varies. Instead use an instant-read thermometer inserted into the side of the burger to determine whether it is done. Shoot for an internal temperature of 160°F for medium doneness.

Bunless Burgers

With a tantalizing mixture of beef and sausage, roasted peppers, and flavor-packed Parmesan, who needs a bun? See photo on page 161.

Prep: 20 minutes **Grill:** 18 minutes **Makes:** 6 servings

2	pounds lean ground beef
8	ounces mild or hot bulk Italian sausage
12	1-inch pieces roasted red sweet peppers
3	ounces Parmesan cheese, cut into $1 \times \frac{1}{4}$-inch slices
	Salt and black pepper
	Iceberg lettuce
6	pear or cherry tomatoes (optional)

1. In a large bowl combine ground beef and sausage. Shape meat mixture into 12 evenly sized balls. On waxed paper, pat each ball into a flat patty 4 inches in diameter. Place one piece of roasted pepper in the center of 6 of the patties; top with Parmesan cheese slices and the remaining roasted pepper pieces. Top with the remaining meat patties to make 6 burgers. Press gently to seal edges. Season with salt and black pepper.

2. For a charcoal grill, arrange medium-hot coals around a drip pan. Test for medium heat above pan. Place burgers on grill rack over drip pan. Cover and grill for 18 to 22 minutes or until done (160°F). (For a gas grill, preheat grill. Reduce heat to medium. Adjust for indirect cooking. Grill as above.)

3. To serve, place each burger between lettuce leaves. If desired, use toothpicks to attach a tomato to each.

Per serving: 391 cal., 26 g total fat (11 g sat. fat), 107 mg chol., 604 mg sodium, 2 g carbo., 0 g fiber, 33 g pro.
Daily Values: 2% vit. A, 86% vit. C, 19% calcium, 15% iron

Hamburgers with Squished Tomato Topper

See photo on page 161.

Prep: 10 minutes **Grill:** 14 minutes **Makes:** 4 servings

1½ pounds lean ground beef

2 ripe tomatoes, peeled and seeded

2 teaspoons olive oil

2 teaspoons balsamic vinegar

Salt and black pepper

4 hamburger buns, split and toasted

1. Shape ground beef into four ¾-inch-thick patties.

2. For a charcoal grill, grill burgers on the rack of an uncovered grill directly over medium coals for 14 to 18 minutes or until done (160°F), turning once halfway through grilling. (For a gas grill, preheat grill. Reduce heat to medium. Place burgers on grill rack over heat. Cover and grill as above.)

3. Meanwhile, for tomato topper, in a medium bowl mash tomatoes with a fork. Stir in olive oil and vinegar. Season to taste with salt and pepper. If desired, line buns with *lettuce leaves*. Serve burgers on buns with tomato topper.

Per serving: 429 cal., 20 g total fat (7 g sat. fat), 107 mg chol., 416 mg sodium, 25 g carbo., 2 g fiber, 35 g pro.
Daily Values: 10% vit. A, 13% vit. C, 8% calcium, 26% iron

Gorgonzola-Garlic-Stuffed Burgers

These juicy burgers are an Italian trifecta of Gorgonzola, basil, and garlic. See photo on page 161.

Prep: 20 minutes **Grill:** 14 minutes **Makes:** 4 servings

- ½ cup crumbled Gorgonzola cheese or other blue cheese
- ¼ cup snipped fresh basil
- 1 teaspoon clove garlic, minced
- 1¼ pounds lean ground beef
  Salt and black pepper
- 4 kaiser rolls, split and toasted
- 1½ cups arugula or fresh spinach leaves (optional)
- 1 large tomato, sliced (optional)

1. In a small bowl combine Gorgonzola cheese, basil, and garlic; shape into 4 slightly flattened mounds. Shape ground beef into eight ¼-inch-thick patties. Place a cheese mound in the center of 4 of the patties. Top with the remaining patties; press gently to seal edges. Season with salt and pepper.

2. For a charcoal grill, grill burgers on the rack of an uncovered grill directly over medium coals for 14 to 18 minutes or until meat is done (160°F), turning once halfway through grilling. (For a gas grill, preheat grill. Reduce heat to medium. Place burgers on grill rack over heat. Cover and grill as above.)

3. Serve burgers on kaiser rolls with, if desired, arugula and tomato.

Per serving: 448 cal., 20 g total fat (8 g sat. fat), 100 mg chol., 704 mg sodium, 31 g carbo., 1 g fiber, 34 g pro.
Daily Values: 5% vit. A, 1% vit. C, 14% calcium, 25% iron

Bayou Burgers

Prep: 25 minutes **Grill:** 14 minutes **Makes:** 6 servings

2 pounds lean ground beef

2 teaspoons Cajun seasoning

½ teaspoon salt

1 cup finely chopped onion and/or green sweet pepper

½ cup shredded Monterey Jack cheese

6 hamburger buns, split and toasted

1. In a large bowl combine ground beef, Cajun seasoning, and salt. Shape beef mixture into 12 thin 3½-inch patties.

2. Combine onion and/or sweet pepper and cheese. Spoon about ¼ cup of the cheese mixture onto the center of 6 of the patties. Top with the remaining patties. Press gently to seal edges.

3. For a charcoal grill, grill burgers on the rack of an uncovered grill directly over medium coals for 14 to 18 minutes or until meat is done (160°F), turning once halfway through grilling. (For a gas grill, preheat grill. Reduce heat to medium. Place burgers on grill rack over heat. Cover and grill as above.) Serve burgers on buns.

Per serving: 413 cal., 19 g total fat (8 g sat. fat), 104 mg chol., 566 mg sodium, 25 g carbo., 1 g fiber, 34 g pro.
Daily Values: 1% vit. A, 3% vit. C, 15% calcium, 24% iron

Bull's-Eye Burgers

Not only are these scrumptious burgers shaped with a bull's-eye on top, they're tastefully targeted to hit the spot. See photo on page 162.

Prep: 20 minutes **Grill:** 10 minutes **Makes:** 4 servings

    1 pound lean ground beef
    1½ teaspoons garlic powder
    ½ teaspoon salt
    ¼ teaspoon black pepper
    1 large sweet onion (such as Vidalia or Maui)
    8 red and/or green kale leaves, stems removed, or other desired lettuce (optional)
    2 teaspoons olive oil (optional)
    4 ¾-inch-thick slices hearty bread or Texas toast, toasted
    4 1-ounce slices Swiss cheese

1. Shape ground beef into four ½-inch-thick patties; sprinkle with garlic powder, salt, and pepper. Cut onion into four ¼-inch-thick slices; reserve remaining onion for another use. Press 1 onion slice into the center of each patty and shape meat around onion until top of onion is flush with the surface of the patty.

2. For a charcoal grill, grill burgers, onion sides up, on the rack of an uncovered grill directly over medium coals for 10 to 13 minutes or until meat is done (160°F), turning once halfway through grilling. If desired, brush kale leaves with oil and add to grill during the last 1½ minutes of grilling. (For a gas grill, preheat grill. Reduce heat to medium. Place burgers on grill rack over heat. Cover and grill as above.)

3. To serve, if desired, place 2 kale leaves on each bread slice. Top each with a slice of cheese and burger, onion side up.

Per serving: 431 cal., 22 g total fat (9 g sat. fat), 148 mg chol., 627 mg sodium, 26 g carbo., 1 g fiber, 34 g pro.
Daily Values: 5% vit. A, 4% vit. C, 28% calcium, 20% iron

Mediterranean Lamb Burgers

See photo on page 162.

Prep: 15 minutes **Grill:** 14 minutes **Makes:** 4 servings

- 1 pound lean ground lamb or beef
- ½ to 1 teaspoon black pepper
- 4 kaiser rolls, split and toasted, or 2 pita bread rounds, halved crosswise
- 4 lettuce leaves
- 2 ounces crumbled feta cheese
- 1 tablespoon snipped fresh mint
-   Chopped tomato (optional)

1. Shape lamb into four ¾-inch-thick patties. Sprinkle pepper evenly over patties; press into patties with your fingers.

2. For a charcoal grill, grill burgers on the rack of an uncovered grill directly over medium coals for 14 to 18 minutes or until meat is done (160°F), turning once halfway through grilling. (For a gas grill, preheat grill. Reduce heat to medium. Place burgers on grill rack over heat. Cover and grill as above.)

3. Serve burgers on rolls with lettuce, feta cheese, mint, and, if desired, tomato.

Per serving: 428 cal., 21 g total fat (9 g sat. fat), 88 mg chol., 533 mg sodium, 31 g carbo., 1 g fiber, 27 g pro.
Daily Values: 2% vit. A, 2% vit. C, 15% calcium, 21% iron

Grilling Juicy Burgers

Here are a few hints to help ensure that your burgers grill up as juicy and flavorful as possible:

- Avoid extremely lean ground beef—fat content of 15 to 20 percent is ideal.

- Don't overwork the meat when shaping patties—quickly and gently pat the meat into shape.

- While grilling, don't smash the burgers with your spatula! Pushing down on burgers squeezes out valuable juices.

Cheese-Stuffed Knockwurst

Sizzling bacon wrapped around juicy sausages stuffed with onions and melted Monterey Jack cheese—add a cold brew and you have your own German feast!

Prep: 15 minutes **Grill:** 8 minutes **Makes:** 5 servings

   5 cooked knockwurst or cooked bratwurst

   2 ounces Monterey Jack cheese or caraway Havarti, cut into five 2½ × ½ × ¼-inch strips

   ¼ cup thinly sliced green onion

   5 slices bacon

   5 frankfurter buns, split and toasted

      Assorted condiments (such as ketchup, yellow mustard, and/or pickle relish) (optional)

1. Cut a lengthwise slit in each knockwurst about ½-inch deep. Insert a cheese strip and some of the green onion into each knockwurst. Wrap a slice of bacon around each knockwurst; secure bacon with wooden toothpicks.

2. For a charcoal grill, arrange medium-hot coals around a drip pan. Test for medium heat above pan. Place knockwurst, cheese side up, on grill rack over drip pan. Cover and grill for 8 to 10 minutes or until bacon is crisp. (For a gas grill, preheat grill. Reduce heat to medium. Adjust for indirect cooking. Grill as above.)

3. Serve knockwurst in buns with, if desired, assorted condiments.

Per serving: 473 cal., 34 g total fat (13 g sat. fat), 77 mg chol., 1,129 mg sodium, 21 g carbo., 1 g fiber, 19 g pro.
Daily Values: 5% vit. C, 15% calcium, 13% iron

Firecracker Foot-Longs

The killer marinade for these fabulous foot-longs will set off a real bang in your mouth. See photo on page 163.

Prep: 10 minutes **Marinate:** 2 to 24 hours **Grill:** 3 minutes **Makes:** 4 servings

    4 foot-long or bun-length frankfurters
    1 5-ounce bottle hot pepper sauce
    ⅓ cup finely chopped red onion
    1 teaspoon dried oregano, crushed
    4 frankfurter buns, split and toasted

1. Place frankfurters in a resealable plastic bag set in a shallow dish. For marinade, combine hot pepper sauce, onion, and oregano. Pour over frankfurters; seal bag. Marinate in refrigerator for 2 to 24 hours, turning bag occasionally.

2. Drain frankfurters, reserving marinade. For a charcoal grill, grill frankfurters on the rack of an uncovered grill directly over medium coals for 3 to 7 minutes or until heated through, turning once halfway through grilling. (For a gas grill, preheat grill. Reduce heat to medium. Place frankfurters on grill rack over heat. Cover and grill as above.)

3. Meanwhile, heat reserved marinade until bubbly. Serve frankfurters in buns with some of the marinade. If desired, top with *pickle relish* and serve with *potato chips* and/or *watermelon slices*.

Per serving: 477 cal., 34 g total fat (13 g sat. fat), 57 mg chol., 2,420 mg sodium, 25 g carbo., 4 g fiber, 18 g pro. Daily Values: 4% vit. A, 45% vit. C, 8% calcium, 17% iron

Hot Dogs with Bacon-Brown Sugar Mustard

Prep: 10 minutes **Chill:** 8 to 48 hours **Grill:** 3 minutes **Makes:** 12 servings

- ¾ cup yellow mustard
- 3 slices bacon, crisp-cooked, drained, and finely crumbled
- 4 teaspoons brown sugar
- 12 frankfurters
- 12 frankfurter buns, split and toasted
- Assorted condiments (such as ketchup, chopped pickled peppers, chopped tomatoes, and/or pickle relish) (optional)

1. For mustard, in a small bowl combine mustard, bacon, and brown sugar. Cover and chill for 8 to 48 hours.

2. For a charcoal grill, grill frankfurters on the rack of an uncovered grill directly over medium coals for 3 to 7 minutes or until heated through, turning once halfway through grilling. (For a gas grill, preheat grill. Reduce heat to medium. Place frankfurters on grill rack over heat. Cover and grill as above.)

3. Serve frankfurters in buns with mustard and, if desired, assorted condiments.

Per serving: 418 cal., 29 g total fat (11 g sat. fat), 50 mg chol., 1,391 mg sodium, 23 g carbo., 2 g fiber, 15 g pro.
Daily Values: 1% vit. C, 7% calcium, 15% iron

Italian Sausage and Pepper Sandwiches

Forget kitchen cleanup—from onions and peppers to Italian sausages and toasted rolls, everything's prepared on your trusty backyard grill.

Prep: 15 minutes **Grill:** 20 minutes **Makes:** 4 servings

  2 medium green, red, and/or yellow sweet peppers, cut into very thin strips (2 cups)
½ cup chopped onion
  3 tablespoons bottled Italian salad dressing
  4 uncooked hot or mild Italian sausage links
  4 hoagie buns, split and toasted

1. Fold a 36×18-inch piece of heavy foil in half to make an 18-inch square. Toss together sweet pepper and onion; mound pepper mixture in center of foil; drizzle with salad dressing. Bring up two opposite edges of foil; seal with a double fold. Fold remaining ends together to completely enclose the sweet pepper mixture, leaving space for steam to build.

2. For a charcoal grill, arrange medium-hot coals around a drip pan. Test for medium heat above pan. Place sausage links and foil packet on grill rack over drip pan. Cover and grill for 20 to 30 minutes or until sausage juices run clear (160°F), turning sausage and foil packet once halfway through grilling. (For a gas grill, preheat grill. Reduce heat to medium. Adjust for indirect grilling. Cover and grill as above.)

3. Serve sausage links in buns; top with pepper mixture.

Per serving: 661 cal., 35 g total fat (11 g sat. fat), 65 mg chol., 1,497 mg sodium, 63 g carbo., 5 g fiber, 23 g pro.
Daily Values: 4% vit. A, 85% vit. C, 13% calcium, 24% iron

Brats Deluxe

Prep: 15 minutes **Grill:** 20 minutes **Cook:** 20 minutes **Makes:** 10 servings

- 10 uncooked bratwurst
- 2 medium onions, halved and thinly sliced
- 1 tablespoon cooking oil
- 1 32-ounce jar sauerkraut, undrained
- 1 12-ounce can beer
- 10 hoagie buns, split and toasted (optional)
- Mustard (optional)

1. Use the tines of a fork to pierce the skin of each bratwurst in several places. For a charcoal grill, arrange medium-hot coals around a drip pan. Test for medium heat above the pan. Place bratwurst on grill rack over drip pan. Cover and grill for 20 to 30 minutes or until bratwurst juices run clear (160°F), turning once halfway through grilling. (For a gas grill, preheat grill. Reduce heat to medium. Adjust for indirect cooking. Grill as above.)

2. Meanwhile, in a Dutch oven cook onion in hot oil until tender. Stir in undrained sauerkraut and beer. Bring to boiling; reduce heat. Simmer, uncovered, for 20 minutes. Add grilled bratwurst; heat through.

3. If desired, serve bratwurst in buns with mustard. Serve with sauerkraut mixture.

Per serving: 311 cal., 23 g total fat (10 g sat. fat), 50 mg chol., 1,262 mg sodium, 8 g carbo., 2 g fiber, 17 g pro.
Daily Values: 1% vit. A, 25% vit. C, 4% calcium, 14% iron

Double Brats 'n' Beer

What's the only thing better than smoky brats hot off the grill? Jam the smoky brats two-in-a-bun!

Prep: 10 minutes **Grill:** 20 minutes **Makes:** 5 servings

 10 uncooked bratwurst

  1 12-ounce can beer

 ¼ cup butter or margarine

  1 large onion, sliced and separated into rings

  5 hoagie or bratwurst buns, split and toasted

    Coarse-ground horseradish mustard and/or pickles (optional)

1. Use the tines of a fork to pierce the skin of each bratwurst in several places. For a charcoal grill, arrange medium-hot coals around a drip pan. Test for medium heat above pan. Place bratwurst on grill rack over drip pan. Cover and grill for 20 to 30 minutes or until bratwurst juices run clear (160°F), turning once halfway through grilling. (For a gas grill, preheat grill. Reduce heat to medium. Adjust for indirect cooking. Grill as above.)

2. Meanwhile, in a Dutch oven combine beer, butter, and onion rings. Bring to boiling; reduce heat. Add grilled bratwurst to beer mixture; heat through.

3. Serve two bratwurst in each bun. If desired, serve with mustard and pickles.

Per serving: 1,046 cal., 59 g total fat (28 g sat. fat), 124 mg chol., 2,072 mg sodium, 82 g carbo., 4 g fiber, 44 g pro.
Daily Values: 8% vit. A, 5% vit. C, 13% calcium, 34% iron

Bratwurst with Kickin' Cranberry Ketchup

See photo on page 164.

Prep: 20 minutes **Grill:** 3 minutes **Makes:** 6 servings

- ¼ cup dried cranberries, coarsely chopped
- ⅓ cup ketchup
- 2 teaspoons prepared horseradish
  Several dashes bottled hot pepper sauce (optional)
- 6 cooked smoked bratwurst
- 6 hoagie buns, split and toasted
- 1 cup prepared vinaigrette-style coleslaw (optional)

1. For ketchup, place cranberries in a small bowl. Add enough boiling water to cover; let stand 5 minutes. Drain cranberries, discarding water. Stir in ketchup, horseradish, and, if desired, hot pepper sauce. Set ketchup aside.

2. For a charcoal grill, grill bratwurst on the rack of an uncovered grill directly over medium coals for 3 to 7 minutes or until bratwurst are browned and heated through, turning once halfway through grilling. (For a gas grill, preheat grill. Reduce heat to medium. Place bratwurst on grill rack over heat. Cover and grill as above.)

3. Serve bratwurst in buns; top with ketchup and, if desired, coleslaw.

Per serving: 689 cal., 32 g total fat (10 g sat. fat), 50 mg chol., 1,536 mg sodium, 81 g carbo., 4 g fiber, 21 g pro.
Daily Values: 2% vit. A, 10% vit. C, 10% calcium, 28% iron

Barbecued Pork Chop Sandwiches

Thick chops are the only way to go for these sandwiches. They sear up nicely on the outside, while the insides stay tender and juicy.

Prep: 10 minutes **Grill:** 14 minutes **Makes:** 4 servings

- ⅓ cup bottled chili sauce
- ½ to 1 teaspoon curry powder
- ¼ teaspoon ground cumin
- 3 boneless pork loin chops, cut 1¼ to 1½ inches thick
   Salt and black pepper (optional)
- 4 kaiser rolls, split and toasted

1. For sauce, in a small bowl combine chili sauce, curry powder, and cumin. Set sauce aside.

2. Trim fat from chops. If desired, sprinkle lightly with salt and pepper.

3. For a charcoal grill, grill chops on the rack of an uncovered grill directly over medium coals for 14 to 18 minutes or until chops are slightly pink in center and juices run clear (160°F), turning once halfway through grilling and brushing occasionally with sauce during the last 5 minutes of grilling. (For a gas grill, preheat grill. Reduce heat to medium. Place chops on grill rack over heat. Cover and grill as above.)

4. To serve, thinly slice pork; serve on rolls.

Per serving: 343 cal., 8 g total fat (2 g sat. fat), 58 mg chol., 618 mg sodium, 34 g carbo., 3 g fiber, 30 g pro.
Daily Values: 3% vit. A, 6% vit. C, 8% calcium, 16% iron

Honey-Mustard Pork Tenderloin Sandwiches

Prep: 10 minutes **Grill:** 12 minutes **Makes:** 4 servings

  1 1-pound pork tenderloin
     Black pepper
  2 tablespoons honey
  2 tablespoons Dijon-style mustard
  4 kaiser rolls or hamburger buns, split and toasted
  ¼ cup mayonnaise or salad dressing
  4 tomato slices (optional)

1. Trim fat from tenderloin. Cut tenderloin crosswise into ¾-inch slices; sprinkle with pepper. For glaze, combine honey and mustard; set aside.

2. For a charcoal grill, grill tenderloin slices on the rack of an uncovered grill directly over medium coals for 12 to 15 minutes or until slightly pink in center and juices run clear (160°F), turning and brushing once with glaze halfway through grilling. (For a gas grill, preheat grill. Reduce heat to medium. Place tenderloin slices on grill rack over heat. Cover and grill as above.)

3. Serve tenderloin slices on rolls with mayonnaise and, if desired, tomato slices.

Per serving: 440 cal., 17 g total fat (4 g sat. fat), 78 mg chol., 617 mg sodium, 40 g carbo., 1 g fiber, 31 g pro.
Daily Values: 1% vit. C, 7% calcium, 18% iron

Gas Grill Safety Check

In addition to periodically reviewing your grill's safety manual, be vigilant about the following:

• Watch for gas leaks. Brush soapy water on all joints and fittings—bubbles indicate a leak. Don't light the grill until the leak is fixed.

• Check hoses for cracks and brittleness—replace hoses that show either. Keep hoses away from heat and hot surfaces.

• Follow the safe transport and storage directions on your propane tank. Always remember that tanks can leak or explode if not handled properly.

Texas Rib Sandwiches with Coleslaw

Coleslaw is an indispensable ingredient for this down-home classic. Pick up a creamy- or vinaigrette-based slaw from your supermarket's deli. See photo on page 165.

Prep: 10 minutes **Grill:** 1½ hours **Makes:** 6 servings

  2 pounds boneless pork country-style ribs
  ¾ cup bottled or homemade barbecue sauce
  6 crusty dinner rolls or hamburger buns, split and toasted
    Bottled hot pepper sauce (optional)
  1 cup prepared coleslaw

1. Trim fat from ribs. For a charcoal grill, arrange medium-hot coals around a drip pan. Test for medium heat above pan. Place ribs on grill rack over pan. (Or place ribs in a rib rack; place on grill rack.) Cover and grill for 1½ to 2 hours or until ribs are tender, brushing occasionally with barbecue sauce during the last 10 minutes of grilling. (For a gas grill, preheat grill. Reduce heat to medium. Adjust for indirect cooking. Grill as above.) Remove ribs from grill and brush with the remaining sauce.

2. Thinly slice ribs. To serve, top the roll bottoms with rib slices and, if desired, sprinkle with hot pepper sauce. Spoon coleslaw on top of sandwiches. Add roll tops.

Per serving: 464 cal., 22 g total fat (7 g sat. fat), 89 mg chol., 635 mg sodium, 37 g carbo., 1 g fiber, 28 g pro.
Daily Values: 4% vit. A, 15% vit. C, 6% calcium, 21% iron

Sweet and Spicy Pork Burgers

Prep: 10 minutes **Grill:** 14 minutes **Makes:** 4 servings

- ¼ cup bottled barbecue sauce
- ¼ cup fine dry bread crumbs
- 1 teaspoon seasoned pepper blend
- 1 pound lean ground pork
- 4 hamburger buns or kaiser rolls, split and toasted
  Leaf lettuce (optional)
  Tomato slices (optional)
  Onion slices (optional)

1. In a large bowl combine barbecue sauce, bread crumbs, and seasoned pepper blend. Add ground pork; mix well. Shape pork mixture into four ¾-inch-thick patties.

2. For a charcoal grill, grill burgers on the rack of an uncovered grill directly over medium coals for 14 to 18 minutes or until meat is done (160°F), turning once halfway through grilling. (For a gas grill, preheat grill. Reduce heat to medium. Place burgers on grill rack over heat. Cover and grill as above.)

3. Serve burgers on buns. If desired, top burgers with lettuce, tomato, and onion.

Per serving: 290 cal., 11 g total fat (4 g sat. fat), 53 mg chol., 555 mg sodium, 29 g carbo., 1 g fiber, 19 g pro.
Daily Values: 2% vit. C, 8% calcium, 15% iron

Italian Stuffed Sausage Burgers

Prep: 25 minutes **Grill:** 20 minutes **Makes:** 4 servings

　　¾ cup shredded provolone or mozzarella cheese

　　3 tablespoons tomato paste

　　2 tablespoons snipped fresh basil or oregano or 2 teaspoons
　　　dried basil or oregano, crushed

　　1 clove garlic, minced

1½ pounds bulk pork sausage

　　2 tablespoons finely shredded Parmesan cheese (optional)

1. In a small bowl combine cheese, tomato paste, basil, and garlic; shape into 4 mounds. Shape sausage into eight ¼-inch-thick patties. Place a cheese mound in the center of 4 of the patties. Top with remaining patties. Press gently to seal.

2. For a charcoal grill, arrange medium-hot coals around a drip pan. Test for medium heat above pan. Place burgers on grill rack over drip pan. Cover and grill for 20 to 24 minutes or until meat is done (160°F), turning once halfway through grilling. If desired, sprinkle the Parmesan cheese over the burgers the last minute of grilling. (For a gas grill, preheat grill. Reduce heat to medium. Adjust for indirect cooking. Grill as above.)

Per serving: 522 cal., 38 g total fat (15 g sat. fat), 125 mg chol., 1,005 mg sodium, 3 g carbo., 0 g fiber, 32 g pro.
Daily Values: 7% vit. A, 6% vit. C, 18% calcium, 9% iron

Southwest Chicken Burgers

Jazzed-up with Southwestern-inspired ingredients, chicken burgers are a tasty alternative to the traditional beef burger rhythm.

Prep: 20 minutes **Grill:** 15 minutes **Makes:** 4 servings

    3 tablespoons finely chopped green sweet pepper
    ¾ teaspoon chili powder
    ¼ teaspoon salt
    ¼ teaspoon black pepper
    1 pound uncooked ground chicken
    1 cup shredded Monterey Jack cheese with jalapeño peppers
    4 kaiser rolls, split and toasted
    1 medium avocado, seeded, peeled, and sliced (optional)
      Bottled salsa (optional)

1. In large bowl combine sweet pepper, chili powder, salt, and black pepper. Add ground chicken; mix well. Shape chicken mixture into four ¾-inch-thick patties.

2. For a charcoal grill, grill burgers on the rack of uncovered grill directly over medium coals for 14 to 18 minutes or until no longer pink (170°F), turning once halfway through grilling. Sprinkle each burger with cheese. Grill 1 to 2 minutes more or until cheese melts. (For a gas grill, preheat grill. Reduce heat to medium. Place burgers on grill rack over heat. Cover and grill as above.)

3. Serve burgers on rolls. If desired, top with avocado and salsa.

Per serving: 497 cal., 26 g total fat (6 g sat. fat), 25 mg chol., 683 mg sodium, 31 g carbo., 2 g fiber, 32 g pro.
Daily Values: 8% vit. A, 10% vit. C, 29% calcium, 19% iron

Basil-Chicken Burgers

See photo on page 166.

Prep: 15 minutes **Grill:** 10 minutes **Makes:** 4 servings

¼ cup snipped fresh basil
¼ cup fine dry bread crumbs
4 teaspoons Worcestershire sauce
⅛ teaspoon salt
⅛ teaspoon black pepper
1 pound uncooked ground chicken
8 slices French bread, toasted, or 4 kaiser rolls or hamburger buns, split and toasted
Assorted condiments (such as lettuce leaves, sliced tomato, and/or sliced onion) (optional)

1. In a large bowl combine basil, bread crumbs, Worcestershire sauce, salt, and pepper. Add ground chicken; mix well. Shape chicken mixture into four ½-inch-thick patties. (The mixture may be sticky. If necessary, wet hands to shape patties.)

2. For a charcoal grill, grill burgers on the rack of an uncovered grill directly over medium coals for 10 to 13 minutes or until no longer pink (170°F), turning once halfway through grilling. (For a gas grill, preheat grill. Reduce heat to medium. Place burgers on grill rack over heat. Cover and grill as above.)

3. If desired, line 4 slices French bread with lettuce and tomato. Top with burgers, onion (if desired), and remaining bread slices.

Per serving: 334 cal., 11 g total fat (0 g sat. fat), 0 mg chol., 678 mg sodium, 32 g carbo., 2 g fiber, 25 g pro.
Daily Values: 3% vit. A, 1% vit. C, 8% calcium, 17% iron

Barbecued Turkey Tenderloin Sandwiches

Quick-cooking turkey tenderloins are delectable when direct-grilled over the coals. A very special basting sauce adds to their gobble-ability. See photo on page 166.

Prep: 20 minutes **Grill:** 16 minutes **Makes:** 4 servings

    ½ cup bottled hickory-flavored barbecue sauce
    1 tablespoon tahini (sesame seed paste)
    1 small fresh jalapeño chile pepper, seeded and finely chopped (see tip, page 34)
    2 turkey breast tenderloins
    4 French-style rolls, split and toasted
      Fresh spinach (optional)
      Bottled green salsa (optional)

1. In a small bowl combine barbecue sauce, tahini, and chile pepper. Set aside half of the sauce to use for basting. Reserve remaining sauce until ready to serve.

2. Brush both sides of each turkey tenderloin with basting sauce. For a charcoal grill, grill turkey on the greased rack of an uncovered grill directly over medium coals for 16 to 20 minutes or until turkey is no longer pink (170°F), turning once halfway through grilling. (For a gas grill, preheat grill. Reduce heat to medium. Place turkey on greased grill rack over heat. Cover and grill as above.)

3. Thinly slice the turkey. Serve on rolls with reserved sauce and, if desired, spinach and salsa.

Per serving: 512 cal., 9 g total fat (2 g sat. fat), 68 mg chol., 1,039 mg sodium, 69 g carbo., 5 g fiber, 37 g pro.
Daily Values: 1% vit. A, 3% vit. C, 15% calcium, 28% iron

Foil-Grilled Cheese Sandwiches

Soaking up the flavorful smoke and sizzle of your backyard barbecue, these sandwiches give delicious new meaning to "grilled" cheese.

Prep: 20 minutes **Grill:** 6 minutes **Makes:** 6 servings

- 12 slices firm-textured white or whole wheat bread
- ¼ cup butter or margarine, softened
- ½ of an 8-ounce container whipped cream cheese
- 2 to 4 tablespoons bottled salsa
- 2 cups shredded cheddar cheese
- ¼ cup finely chopped green sweet pepper (optional)

1. Spread 1 side of each bread slice with butter. Spread cream cheese on unbuttered side of 6 of the bread slices. Spoon 1 to 2 teaspoons salsa over cream cheese; sprinkle with cheddar cheese and, if desired, sweet pepper. Top with remaining bread slices, buttered sides up. Press sandwiches down to flatten slightly.

2. For a charcoal grill, grill sandwiches on the foil-covered grill rack of an uncovered grill directly over medium coals about 6 minutes or until browned and cheese is melted, turning once halfway through grilling. (For a gas grill, preheat grill. Reduce heat to medium. Place sandwiches on foil-covered grill rack over heat. Cover and grill as above.)

Per serving: 427 cal., 30 g total fat (17 g sat. fat), 81 mg chol., 631 mg sodium, 27 g carbo., 0 g fiber, 15 g pro.
Daily Values: 18% vit. A, 33% calcium, 11% iron

sauces, rubs & more

Tangy Barbecue Sauce

Great chefs labor for hours, sometimes days, to make a great sauce. You'll have this tantalizing sauce ready in minutes.

Prep: 10 minutes **Cook:** 10 minutes
Makes: about 1½ cups

  1 cup ketchup

  ⅓ cup balsamic vinegar or cider vinegar

  ⅓ cup light-colored corn syrup

  ¼ cup finely chopped onion or thinly sliced green onion

  ¼ teaspoon salt

      Several dashes bottled hot pepper sauce

1. In a small saucepan combine ketchup, vinegar, corn syrup, onion, salt, and hot pepper sauce. Bring to boiling; reduce heat. Simmer, uncovered, for 10 to 15 minutes or until desired consistency, stirring occasionally.

2. To use, brush beef, pork, or poultry with some of the sauce during the last 10 minutes of grilling. If desired, reheat any remaining sauce until bubbly. Pass with meat or poultry.

Per tablespoon: 28 cal., 0 g total fat (0 g sat. fat), 0 mg chol., 140 mg sodium, 7 g carbo., 0 g fiber, 0 g pro.
Daily Values: 2% vit. A, 3% vit. C

Apple Butter Barbecue Sauce

Prep: 5 minutes **Makes:** about 1½ cups

  1 8-ounce can tomato sauce

  ½ cup purchased apple butter

  2 tablespoons light-colored corn syrup (optional)

  1 tablespoon Pickapeppa sauce or Worcestershire sauce

1. In a small saucepan combine tomato sauce, apple butter, corn syrup (if desired), and Pickapeppa sauce. Bring just to boiling; remove from heat.

2. To use, brush pork or poultry with some of the sauce during the last 10 minutes of grilling. If desired, reheat any remaining sauce until bubbly, stirring occasionally. Pass with meat or poultry.

Per tablespoon: 34 cal., 0 g total fat (0 g sat. fat), 0 mg chol., 51 mg sodium, 8 g carbo., 0 g fiber, 0 g pro.
Daily Values: 1% iron

Molasses Barbecue Sauce

Prep: 10 minutes **Makes:** about 1½ cups

- 1 cup ketchup
- ¼ cup full-flavored molasses
- ¼ cup water
- ½ teaspoon finely shredded lemon peel
- 1 tablespoon lemon juice
- 2 teaspoons Worcestershire sauce
- ½ teaspoon black pepper
- ⅛ teaspoon salt

1. In a bowl combine ketchup, molasses, water, lemon peel, lemon juice, Worcestershire sauce, pepper, and salt.

2. To use, brush beef, pork, or poultry with some of the sauce during the last 5 to 10 minutes of grilling. If desired, heat any remaining sauce until bubbly and pass with meat or poultry.

Per tablespoon: 40 cal., 0 g total fat (0 g sat. fat), 0 mg chol., 260 mg sodium, 10 g carbo., 0 g fiber, 0 g pro.
Daily Values: 4% vit. A, 6% vit. C, 2% calcium, 3% iron

Basic Moppin' Sauce

All pitmasters need a go-to sauce that works with a wide range of foods. This one fills the bill and then some.

Prep: 15 minutes **Cook:** 30 minutes
Makes: about 2 cups

- 1 cup strong coffee
- 1 cup ketchup
- ½ cup Worcestershire sauce
- ¼ cup butter or margarine
- 1 tablespoon sugar
- 1 to 2 teaspoons black pepper
- ½ teaspoon salt (optional)

1. In a medium saucepan combine coffee, ketchup, Worcestershire sauce, butter, sugar, pepper, and, if desired, salt. Bring to boiling, stirring occasionally; reduce heat. Simmer, uncovered, for 30 minutes, stirring frequently.

2. To use, brush beef, pork, or poultry with some of the sauce during the last 5 to 10 minutes of grilling. If desired, reheat any remaining sauce until bubbly. Pass with meat or poultry.

Per tablespoon: 25 cal., 1 g total fat (1 g sat. fat), 4 mg chol., 143 mg sodium, 3 g carbo., 0 g fiber, 0 g pro.
Daily Values: 2% vit. A, 2% vit. C, 2% iron

Honey-Peach Sauce

Rich, intense, and slightly sweet, this peach of a sauce pairs perfectly with grilled pork or poultry.

Prep: 5 minutes **Cook:** 15 minutes
Makes: about 1¾ cups

4 medium peaches

2 tablespoons lemon juice

2 tablespoons honey

½ teaspoon cracked black pepper

1 to 2 teaspoons snipped fresh thyme

1. Peel and cut up 3 of the peaches; place in a blender. Add lemon juice, honey, and pepper. Cover and blend until smooth. Transfer to a medium saucepan. Bring to boiling; reduce heat. Simmer, uncovered, about 15 minutes or until slightly thickened, stirring occasionally. Remove from heat. Peel and finely chop the remaining peach; stir into sauce. Stir in thyme.

2. To use, brush pork or poultry with some of the sauce during the last 15 minutes of grilling. If desired, reheat any remaining sauce until bubbly. Pass with pork or poultry.

Per tablespoon: 15 cal., 0 g total fat (0 g sat. fat), 0 mg chol., 0 mg sodium, 4 g carbo., 0 g fiber, 0 g pro.
Daily Values: 3% vit. C

Cucumber-Dill Sauce

Prep: 10 minutes **Makes:** about ⅔ cup

⅓ cup finely chopped, seeded cucumber

3 tablespoons plain yogurt

2 tablespoons mayonnaise or salad dressing

2 teaspoons prepared horseradish

2 teaspoons snipped fresh dill

1. In a small bowl combine cucumber, yogurt, mayonnaise, horseradish, and dill. Serve immediately or cover and chill up to 4 hours.

2. To use, serve with fish.

Per tablespoon: 24 cal., 2 g total fat (0 g sat. fat), 1 mg chol., 21 mg sodium, 1 g carbo., 0 g fiber, 0 g pro.
Daily Values: 1% vit. C, 1% calcium

Yogurt-Mustard Sauce

Balancing tanginess with depth, this sauce shines with grilled lamb or chicken.

Prep: 5 minutes **Chill:** 1 hour
Makes: about ¾ cup

⅔ cup plain yogurt

2 tablespoons lime juice

4 teaspoons Dijon-style mustard

1. In a small bowl combine yogurt, lime juice, and mustard. Cover and chill for 1 hour.

2. To use, serve with lamb or chicken.

Per tablespoon: 11 cal., 0 g total fat (0 g sat. fat),
1 mg chol., 50 mg sodium, 2 g carbo., 0 g fiber, 1 g pro.
Daily Values: 1% vit. C, 3% calcium

Portobello Sauce

Prep: 10 minutes **Makes:** about ¾ cup

2 large fresh portobello mushrooms, halved and sliced

8 green onions, cut into 1-inch pieces

1 tablespoon butter or margarine

⅓ cup beef broth

2 tablespoons Madeira or port wine

1. In a large skillet cook and stir mushrooms and onion in hot butter over medium heat about 5 minutes or until tender. Stir in beef broth and Madeira. Bring to boiling.

2. To use, serve with beef or lamb.

Per ¼ cup: 53 cal., 4 g total fat (2 g sat. fat),
7 mg chol., 84 mg sodium, 4 g carbo., 1 g fiber, 2 g pro.
Daily Values: 3% vit. A, 6% vit C, 2% calcium, 4% iron

Ginger-Orange Brush-On

Prep: 10 minutes **Makes:** about ¾ cup

- ½ cup bottled barbecue sauce
- ¼ cup frozen orange juice concentrate, thawed
- 2 tablespoons soy sauce
- 1 tablespoon grated fresh ginger

1. In a small bowl combine barbecue sauce, orange juice concentrate, soy sauce, and ginger.

2. To use, brush beef, lamb, pork, or poultry with some of the sauce during the last 15 minutes of grilling. If desired, reheat any remaining sauce until bubbly. Pass with meat or poultry.

Per tablespoon: 19 cal., 0 g total fat (0 g sat. fat), 0 mg chol., 238 mg sodium, 4 g carbo., 0 g fiber, 1 g pro.
Daily Values: 1% vit. A, 15% vit. C, 1% calcium, 1% iron

Lemon-Herb Brush-On

Prep: 5 minutes **Makes:** about ⅓ cup

- 2 tablespoons butter or margarine
- 3 tablespoons lemon juice
- 1 teaspoon dried thyme, savory, or sage, crushed
- 3 cloves garlic, minced
- ¼ teaspoon salt
- ¼ teaspoon black pepper

1. In a small saucepan melt the butter; stir in lemon juice, thyme, garlic, salt, and pepper.

2. To use, brush evenly onto pork, poultry, or fish. Brush occasionally with remaining sauce during the first half of grilling. Discard remaining sauce.

Per tablespoon: 49 cal., 5 g total fat (3 g sat. fat), 12 mg chol., 150 mg sodium, 2 g carbo., 0 g fiber, 0 g pro.
Daily Values: 4% vit. A, 8% vit. C, 1% calcium, 1% iron

Bunless Burgers, page 133

Hamburgers with Squished Tomato Topper, page 134

Gorgonzola-Garlic-Stuffed Burgers, page 135

Bull's-Eye Burgers,
page 137

Mediterranean Lamb
Burgers, page 138

Firecracker Foot-Longs, page 140

Bratwurst with Kickin' Cranberry Ketchup, page 145

Texas Rib Sandwiches with Coleslaw, page 148

Basil-Chicken Burgers,
page 152

Barbecued Turkey
Tenderloin Sandwiches,
page 153

Herb-Grilled Tomatoes, page 200

Corn and Tomato Salad, page 205

Italian Breadsticks, page 208

Fill-the-Grill Nectarine Toss,
page 212

Banana Split Kabobs, page 213

**Pineapple Fries
with Raspberry
Ketchup,
page 218**

**Gorgonzola-Walnut-Stuffed Apples,
page 219**

Dessert Burritos, page 220

Deviled Eggs, page 232

Super-Quick Ice Cream Sandwiches,
page 243

Cheese Straws, page 245

Minted Iced Tea,
page 246

Easy Mustard-Beer Brush-On

Prep: 5 minutes **Makes:** about ¼ cup

　3　tablespoons stone-ground mustard

　¾　teaspoon Worcestershire sauce

　1　tablespoon beer

1. In a small bowl combine mustard, Worcestershire sauce, and beer.

2. To use, brush evenly onto burgers, steaks, or poultry during the last 5 minutes of grilling. Or spoon over meat or poultry just before serving.

Per tablespoon: 13 cal., 1 g total fat (0 g sat. fat),
0 mg chol., 166 mg sodium, 1 g carbo., 0 g fiber, 1 g pro.
Daily Values: 1% calcium, 2% iron

Tandoori-Style Brush-On

This rub helps you simulate the distinctive flavor of foods cooked in a tandoor, a traditional Indian-style clay oven.

Prep: 10 minutes **Makes:** about ¼ cup

　2　tablespoons cooking oil

　6　cloves garlic, minced

　2　teaspoons grated fresh ginger

　1　tablespoon garam masala

　½　teaspoon salt

1. In a small bowl combine oil, garlic, ginger, garam masala, and salt.

2. To use, spread evenly over lamb or poultry.

Per tablespoon: 71 cal., 7 g total fat (1 g sat. fat),
0 mg chol., 293 mg sodium, 2 g carbo., 0 g fiber, 0 g pro.
Daily Values: 2% vit. C, 2% calcium, 2% iron

Teriyaki Glaze

Prep: 5 minutes **Cook:** 10 minutes
Makes: about ¼ cup

    3 tablespoons soy sauce

    3 tablespoons sweet rice wine (mirin)

    2 tablespoons dry white wine

    1½ teaspoons sugar

    1½ teaspoons honey

1. In a small saucepan combine soy
sauce, rice wine, white wine, sugar, and
honey. Bring to boiling; reduce heat.
Simmer, uncovered, about 10 minutes or
until glaze is reduced to ¼ cup.

2. To use, brush onto pork, poultry, or
fish during the last 2 minutes of grilling.
Discard any remaining glaze.

Per tablespoon: 29 cal., 0 g total fat (0 g sat. fat),
0 mg chol., 351 mg sodium, 6 g carbo., 0 g fiber, 1 g pro.
Daily Values: 1% vit. A, 1% vit. C, 1% calcium, 1% iron

Mustard-Jalapeño Glaze

Prep: 10 minutes **Makes:** about ½ cup

    3 tablespoons Dijon-style mustard

    1 tablespoon frozen orange juice
      concentrate, thawed

    1 tablespoon light-colored corn syrup

    1 to 2 tablespoons finely chopped
      canned jalapeño chile peppers,
      seeded, if desired

    ½ teaspoon lemon-pepper seasoning

1. In a small bowl combine the
mustard, orange juice concentrate,
corn syrup, jalapeño peppers, and
lemon-pepper seasoning.

2. To use, brush onto beef, pork, or fish
during the last 2 to 3 minutes of grilling.

Per tablespoon: 29 cal., 0 g total fat (0 g sat. fat),
0 mg chol., 442 mg sodium, 7 g carbo., 0 g fiber, 2 g pro.
Daily Values: 3% vit. A, 9% vit. C, 2% calcium, 2% iron

Ginger-Allspice Rub

Lime, along with a heady mélange of spices, makes this the rub of choice for white-fleshed fish.

Prep: 10 minutes
Makes: enough for 1 pound of fish

1 tablespoon lime juice

1 tablespoon water

1 teaspoon paprika

½ teaspoon salt

¼ teaspoon ground ginger

¼ teaspoon ground allspice

¼ teaspoon black pepper

1. In a small bowl combine lime juice and water. For rub, in another small bowl combine paprika, salt, ginger, allspice, and pepper.

2. To use, brush juice mixture onto fish. Sprinkle evenly with rub; rub in with your fingers.

Per teaspoon: 8 cal., 0 g total fat (0 g sat. fat), 0 mg chol., 583 mg sodium, 2 g carbo., 1 g fiber, 0 g pro.
Daily Values: 9% vit. A, 4% vit. C, 1% calcium, 2% iron

Herb Rub

Prep: 10 minutes **Makes:** enough for 5 pounds of beef, pork, poultry, or seafood

2 teaspoons dried rosemary

2 teaspoons dried thyme

2 teaspoons dried minced onion

2 teaspoons dried minced garlic

1 teaspoon salt

¾ teaspoon black pepper

1. In a blender combine rosemary, thyme, onion, garlic, salt, and pepper. Cover and blend until coarsely ground.

2. To use, sprinkle rub evenly over beef, pork, poultry, or seafood; rub in with your fingers.

Per teaspoon: 7 cal., 0 g total fat (0 g sat. fat), 0 mg chol., 233 mg sodium, 1 g carbo., 0 g fiber, 0 g pro.
Daily Values: 1% vit. A, 1% calcium, 2% iron

Mustard-Peppercorn Rub

Prep: 10 minutes
Makes: enough for 3 pounds of meat

- 1 tablespoon coarse-grain brown mustard
- 2 teaspoons olive oil
- 2 teaspoons cracked black pepper
- 2 teaspoons snipped fresh tarragon
- 1 teaspoon coarse salt

1. In a small bowl combine mustard, oil, pepper, tarragon, and salt.

2. To use, spoon rub over beef, lamb, or pork; rub in with your fingers. Cover and chill at least 15 minutes or up to 4 hours.

Per teaspoon: 12 cal., 1 g total fat (0 g sat. fat), 0 mg chol., 237 mg sodium, 0 g carbo., 0 g fiber, 0 g pro.
Daily Values: 1% iron

Horseradish-Pepper Steak Rub

Power-packed with horseradish, garlic, and cracked pepper, this powerful rub is the one to use with flavorful grilled beef steaks.

Prep: 5 minutes
Makes: enough for 6 pounds of steak

- 2 tablespoons cream-style prepared horseradish
- 1 tablespoon cracked black pepper
- 2 teaspoons bottled minced garlic
- ½ teaspoon salt

1. In a small bowl combine horseradish, pepper, garlic, and salt.

2. To use, spoon rub evenly over steaks; rub in with your fingers.

Per teaspoon: 6 cal., 0 g total fat (0 g sat. fat), 0 mg chol., 158 mg sodium, 1 g carbo., 0 g fiber, 0 g pro.
Daily Values: 3% vit. C, 1% calcium, 1% iron

Balsamic-Mustard Marinade

Not only does this recipe add loads of flavor when used as a marinade, but it makes a killer brush-on sauce as well.

Prep: 5 minutes **Makes:** enough for 3 pounds of meat or poultry

- ¼ cup Dijon-style mustard
- ¼ cup balsamic vinegar
- 2 teaspoons cracked black pepper

1. In a small bowl combine mustard, vinegar, and pepper.

2. To use, pour over beef, pork, or poultry in a resealable plastic bag; seal bag. Marinate in refrigerator for 2 to 4 hours, turning bag occasionally. Drain meat or poultry, discarding marinade.

Per tablespoon: 19 cal., 0 g total fat (0 g sat. fat), 0 mg chol., 182 mg sodium, 4 g carbo., 0 g fiber, 2 g pro.
Daily Values: 1% calcium, 2% iron

Mango Mayonnaise

Prep: 10 minutes **Chill:** up to 24 hours
Makes: about ¾ cup

- ½ cup finely chopped, peeled mango
- ¼ cup mayonnaise or light mayonnaise dressing
- 2 teaspoons lime juice

1. In a small bowl combine mango, mayonnaise, and lime juice. Cover and chill for up to 24 hours.

2. To use, serve with pork, poultry, or fish.

Per tablespoon: 38 cal., 4 g total fat (1 g sat. fat), 2 mg chol., 25 mg sodium, 1 g carbo., 0 g fiber, 0 g pro.
Daily Values: 5% vit. A, 4% vit. C

Curry Mayonnaise

Prep: 10 minutes **Chill:** up to 24 hours
Makes: about ½ cup

- ¼ cup mayonnaise or salad dressing
- ¼ cup dairy sour cream
- 2 tablespoons frozen orange juice concentrate
- ¾ to 1 teaspoon curry powder
- 4 to 5 tablespoons milk

1. In a small bowl combine mayonnaise, sour cream, orange juice concentrate, and curry powder. Stir in enough milk to make drizzling consistency. Cover and chill up to 24 hours.

2. To use, serve with poultry or fish.

Per tablespoon: 74 cal., 7 g total fat (2 g sat. fat), 6 mg chol., 44 mg sodium, 2 g carbo., 0 g fiber, 1 g pro.
Daily Values: 1% vit. A, 10% vit. C, 2% calcium

Garlic-Mustard Mayonnaise

Prep: 5 minutes **Chill:** up to 24 hours
Makes: ⅓ cup

- ⅓ cup mayonnaise or salad dressing
- 1 tablespoon coarse-grain brown mustard
- 2 cloves garlic, minced

1. In a small bowl combine mayonnaise, mustard, and garlic. Cover and chill for up to 24 hours.

2. To use, serve with beef, pork, lamb, or ham.

Per tablespoon: 111 cal., 12 g total fat (2 g sat. fat), 5 mg chol., 126 mg sodium, 1 g carbo., 0 g fiber, 0 g pro.
Daily Values: 1% vit. C, 1% calcium

Herbed Mayonnaise

Prep: 10 minutes **Chill:** up to 24 hours
Makes: about 1¼ cups

- ½ **cup mayonnaise or salad dressing**
- ½ **cup dairy sour cream**
- 3 **tablespoons snipped fresh dill**
- 2 **tablespoons snipped fresh parsley**
- 1 **clove garlic, minced**

1. In a food processor or blender combine mayonnaise, sour cream, dill, parsley, and garlic. Cover and process or blend until almost smooth. Transfer to a small bowl. Cover and chill for up to 24 hours.

2. To use, serve with beef, lamb, pork, poultry, or fish.

Per tablespoon: 51 cal., 5 g total fat (1 g sat. fat), 4 mg chol., 33 mg sodium, 0 g carbo., 0 g fiber, 0 g pro. **Daily Values:** 1% vit. A, 1% vit. C, 1% calcium

Jalapeño Mayo

Prep: 10 minutes **Chill:** up to 24 hours
Makes: about ⅓ cup

- ⅓ **cup mayonnaise or salad dressing**
- 1 **fresh jalapeño chile pepper, seeded and finely chopped (see tip, page 34)**
- 1 **tablespoon Dijon-style mustard**
- 1 **teaspoon lemon juice**

1. In a small bowl combine mayonnaise, jalapeño pepper, mustard, and lemon juice. Cover and chill up to 24 hours.

2. To use, serve with fish or seafood.

Per tablespoon: 91 cal., 10 g total fat (2 g sat. fat), 4 mg chol., 126 mg sodium, 1 g carbo., 0 g fiber, 1 g pro. **Daily Values:** 2% vit. C

Tomato Aïoli

Prep: 10 minutes **Chill:** up to 24 hours
Makes: ⅔ cup

- ½ cup mayonnaise or salad dressing
- 2 tablespoons oil-packed dried tomatoes, drained and finely chopped
- 1 tablespoon snipped fresh basil
- 1 teaspoon snipped fresh thyme
- 1 teaspoon bottled minced garlic

1. In a small bowl combine mayonnaise, tomatoes, basil, thyme, and garlic. Cover and chill for up to 24 hours.

2. To use, serve with poultry or fish.

Per tablespoon: 84 cal., 9 g total fat (1 g sat. fat), 8 mg chol., 72 mg sodium, 1 g carbo., 0 g fiber, 0 g pro.
Daily Values: 1% vit. A, 3% vit. C

Mango Salsa

The bright flavors of Mango Salsa complement all sorts of foods on the lighter end of the scale, from fish and seafood to poultry.

Prep: 20 minutes **Chill:** 2 to 24 hours
Makes: 2½ cups

- 2 cups chopped, peeled mango
- 1 cup chopped red sweet pepper
- ¼ cup snipped fresh cilantro
- 2 tablespoons lime juice
- ⅛ teaspoon cayenne pepper

1. In a small bowl combine mango, sweet pepper, cilantro, lime juice, and cayenne pepper. Cover and chill for 2 to 24 hours.

2. To use, serve with poultry, fish, or seafood.

Per ¼ cup: 27 cal., 0 g total fat (0 g sat. fat), 0 mg chol., 2 mg sodium, 7 g carbo., 1 g fiber, 0 g pro.
Daily Values: 45% vit. A, 65% vit. C, 1% calcium, 1% iron

Papaya Salsa

Prep: 20 minutes **Chill:** 2 to 24 hours
Makes: about 2 cups

> 1 fresh serrano chile pepper, seeded and finely chopped (see tip, page 34)
>
> 1⅓ cups coarsely chopped, peeled, and seeded papaya or mango
>
> ⅔ cup chopped red sweet pepper and/or chopped peeled jicama
>
> 2 tablespoons pineapple juice or orange juice
>
> 1 tablespoon snipped fresh cilantro or parsley

1. In a small bowl combine serrano pepper, papaya, sweet pepper, pineapple juice, and cilantro. Cover and chill for 2 to 24 hours.

2. To use, serve with poultry, fish, or seafood.

Per ¼ cup: 18 cal., 0 g total fat (0 g sat. fat), 0 mg chol., 2 mg sodium, 4 g carbo., 1 g fiber, 0 g pro.
Daily Values: 10% vit. A, 67% vit. C, 1% calcium, 1% iron

Grilled Sweet Pepper Relish

Prep: 10 minutes **Grill:** 8 minutes
Makes: 4 servings

> 1 medium onion, thinly sliced
>
> 1 red or yellow sweet pepper, cut into strips
>
> 1 tablespoon red wine vinegar
>
> 2 teaspoons olive oil
>
> ⅛ teaspoon black pepper

1. Fold a 24×18-inch piece of heavy foil in half to make a 12×18-inch rectangle. Place onion and sweet pepper in center of foil. Drizzle vinegar and oil over the onion and sweet pepper; sprinkle with black pepper. Bring up opposite edges of the foil and seal with a double fold. Fold remaining edges together to completely enclose the vegetables, leaving space for steam to build.

2. For a charcoal grill, grill foil packet on the rack of an uncovered grill directly over medium coals for 8 minutes, turning packet once halfway through grilling. (For a gas grill, preheat grill. Reduce heat to medium. Place foil packet on grill rack over heat. Cover and grill as above.)

3. Serve with pork or poultry.

Per serving: 36 cal., 2 g total fat (0 g sat. fat), 0 mg chol., 1 mg sodium, 4 g carbo., 1 g fiber, 1 g pro.
Daily Values: 32% vit. A, 82% vit. C, 1% calcium, 1% iron

Pineapple Relish

Prep: 15 minutes **Chill:** 2 to 24 hours
Stand: 30 minutes **Makes:** 2 cups

1 cup chopped fresh pineapple

½ cup chopped red sweet pepper

¼ cup chopped green onion

3 tablespoons snipped fresh cilantro

½ to 1 fresh jalapeño chile pepper,
    seeded and finely chopped (see tip,
    page 34)

1. In a small bowl combine the pineapple, sweet pepper, green onion, cilantro, and jalapeño pepper. Cover and chill for 2 to 24 hours.

2. To use, let stand at room temperature for 30 minutes. Serve with pork, ham, or fish.

Per tablespoon: 4 cal., 0 g total fat (0 g sat. fat), 0 mg chol., 1 mg sodium, 1 g carbo., 0 g fiber, 0 g pro.
Daily Values: 3% vit. A, 9% vit. C

Pesto Butter

Prep: 10 minutes **Makes:** about ⅓ cup

3 tablespoons butter, softened

3 tablespoons purchased basil pesto

2 tablespoons chopped walnuts,
    toasted

2 tablespoons finely chopped
    kalamata olives (optional)

1. In a small bowl combine butter, pesto, walnuts, and, if desired, olives. Serve immediately or cover and chill until serving time. Let stand at room temperature 30 minutes before serving, if chilled. To use, serve with poultry or fish.

Per tablespoon: 157 cal., 16 g total fat (7 g sat. fat), 27 mg chol., 166 mg sodium, 2 g carbo., 1 g fiber, 2 g pro.
Daily Values: 7% vit. A, 4% calcium, 1% iron

Blue Cheese Butter

Prep: 10 minutes **Makes:** ½ cup

- ¼ cup butter, softened
- ¼ cup crumbled blue cheese
- 1 tablespoon snipped fresh parsley
- 2 teaspoons snipped fresh basil
- 1 clove garlic, minced

1. In a small bowl combine butter, blue cheese, parsley, basil, and garlic. Serve immediately or cover and chill until serving time. Let stand at room temperature 30 minutes before serving, if chilled. To use, serve with beef.

Per tablespoon: 67 cal., 7 g total fat (4 g sat. fat), 18 mg chol., 100 mg sodium, 0 g carbo., 0 g fiber, 1 g pro.
Daily Values: 5% vit. A, 1% vit. C, 3% calcium

Citrus Butter

Made for melting on meat, fish, and vegetables, a compound butter such as this is one of the easiest ways to make a luxuriously rich sauce.

Prep: 10 minutes **Makes:** ½ cup

- ½ cup butter, softened
- 2 tablespoons snipped fresh parsley
- 1 tablespoon finely shredded lemon peel
- 1 tablespoon finely shredded orange peel
- 1 clove garlic, minced

1. In a small bowl combine butter, parsley, lemon peel, orange peel, and garlic. Serve immediately or cover and chill until serving time. Let stand at room temperature 30 minutes before serving, if chilled. To use, serve with fish or seafood.

Per tablespoon: 103 cal., 12 g total fat (7 g sat. fat), 31 mg chol., 82 mg sodium, 1 g carbo., 0 g fiber, 0 g pro.
Daily Values: 9% vit. A, 6% vit. C, 1% calcium

Basil Butter

Prep: 10 minutes **Makes:** ⅓ cup

  ⅓ cup butter, softened

  1 tablespoon snipped fresh basil or
    ¼ teaspoon dried basil, crushed

  ¼ teaspoon black pepper

  1 clove garlic, minced

1. In a small bowl combine butter, basil, pepper, and garlic. Serve immediately or cover and chill until serving time. Let stand at room temperature 30 minutes before serving, if chilled. To use, serve with beef, lamb, poultry, or fish.

Per tablespoon: 115 cal., 13 g total fat (8 g sat. fat), 35 mg chol., 131 mg sodium, 0 g carbo., 0 g fiber, 0 g pro.
Daily Values: 10% vit. A, 1% vit. C, 1% calcium

Tomato-Garlic Butter

Prep: 15 minutes **Makes:** ½ cup

  ½ cup butter, softened

  1 tablespoon finely snipped oil-packed
    dried tomatoes, drained

  1 tablespoon chopped kalamata olives

  1 tablespoon finely chopped
    green onion

  1 clove garlic, minced

1. In a small bowl combine butter, tomatoes, olives, green onion, and garlic. Serve immediately or cover and chill until serving time. Let stand at room temperature 30 minutes before serving, if chilled. To use, serve with beef or lamb.

Per tablespoon: 112 cal., 12 g total fat (8 g sat. fat), 33 mg chol., 138 mg sodium, 0 g carbo., 0 g fiber, 0 g pro.
Daily Values: 9% vit. A, 2% vit. C, 1% calcium, 1% iron

sides & desserts

Apple-Raisin Baked Beans

Baked beans, a classic summertime dish, gets a deliciously creative fix-up with the additions of chopped apple and raisins.

Prep: 10 minutes **Grill:** 15 minutes **Makes:** 6 to 8 side-dish servings

    2 16-ounce cans vegetarian baked beans, undrained
    1 Granny Smith or other cooking apple, peeled, cored, and chopped
    ¼ to ½ cup raisins
    1 tablespoon minced dried onion (optional)

1. Combine the undrained beans, apple, raisins, and, if desired, the dried onion in a disposable foil pan.

2. For a charcoal grill, grill foil pan on the rack of an uncovered grill directly over medium coals about 15 minutes or until bean mixture is heated through, stirring once or twice. (For a gas grill, preheat grill. Reduce heat to medium. Place foil pan on grill rack over heat. Cover and grill as above.)

Per serving: 172 cal., 1 g total fat (0 g sat. fat), 0 mg chol., 510 mg sodium, 40 g carbo., 7 g fiber, 7 g pro.
Daily Values: 4% vit. A, 2% vit. C, 6% calcium, 11% iron

Summer Squash with Cheese

Prep: 10 minutes **Grill:** 8 minutes **Makes:** 6 side-dish servings

    3 small yellow summer squash or zucchini (about 12 ounces)
    2 teaspoons cooking oil
    ¼ teaspoon salt
    ⅛ teaspoon black pepper
    3 tablespoons bottled picante sauce
    ¼ cup shredded Monterey Jack cheese
    1 tablespoon snipped fresh cilantro

1. Trim ends from squash; halve squash lengthwise. Brush squash with oil; sprinkle cut surfaces with salt and pepper.

2. For a charcoal grill, grill squash on the rack of an uncovered grill directly over medium coals for 8 to 10 minutes or until crisp-tender, turning once halfway through grilling and brushing occasionally with picante sauce. (For a gas grill, preheat grill. Reduce heat to medium. Place squash on grill rack over heat. Cover and grill as above.)

3. To serve, transfer squash to a serving platter; sprinkle with cheese and cilantro.

Per serving: 43 cal., 3 g total fat (1 g sat. fat), 4 mg chol., 176 mg sodium, 3 g carbo., 1 g fiber, 2 g pro.
Daily Values: 4% vit. A, 16% vit. C, 5% calcium, 2% iron

Sweet Peppers Stuffed with Goat Cheese and Herbs

Prep: 15 minutes **Grill:** 5 minutes **Makes:** 4 side-dish servings

- 2 medium red, yellow, or green sweet peppers
- 1 ounce soft goat cheese (chèvre)
- ¼ cup shredded Monterey Jack cheese
- 1 tablespoon snipped fresh chives
- 1 tablespoon snipped fresh basil

1. Cut sweet peppers in half lengthwise. Remove and discard seeds and membranes. Cook peppers, covered, in a small amount of boiling water for 2 minutes. Drain sweet peppers, cut sides down, on paper towels.

2. Meanwhile, in a small bowl combine goat cheese, Monterey Jack cheese, chives, and basil. Divide cheese mixture evenly among sweet pepper halves.

3. Tear off a 24×18-inch piece of heavy foil; fold in half to make a 12×18-inch rectangle. Place filled sweet peppers in center of foil rectangle. Bring up two opposite edges of foil; seal with a double fold. Fold remaining edges together to completely enclose peppers, leaving space for steam to build.

4. For a charcoal grill, grill foil packet on the rack of an uncovered grill directly over medium coals for 5 to 6 minutes or until peppers are crisp-tender and cheese is melted. (For a gas grill, preheat grill. Reduce heat to medium. Place foil packet on grill rack over heat. Cover and grill as above.)

Per serving: 60 cal., 4 g total fat (2 g sat. fat), 13 mg chol., 80 mg sodium, 3 g carbo., 0 g fiber, 3 g pro.
Daily Values: 104% vit. C, 4% calcium

Buttered Rosemary New Potatoes

Do you want to make the buttery-sweet flavor of roasted new potatoes even better? Try cooking them over the coals!

Prep: 10 minutes **Grill:** 30 minutes **Makes:** 4 side-dish servings

1 pound tiny new potatoes, halved

2 tablespoons butter or margarine, melted

1 tablespoon snipped fresh chives

2 teaspoons snipped fresh rosemary or ½ teaspoon dried rosemary, crushed

⅛ teaspoon chili powder

Salt and black pepper

1. Place potatoes in a greased disposable foil pan. Combine melted butter, chives, rosemary, and chili powder; pour over potatoes, tossing to coat.

2. For a charcoal grill, arrange hot coals around edge of grill. Test for medium-hot heat above center of grill. Place foil pan on grill rack over center of grill. Cover and grill for 30 to 35 minutes or until potatoes are tender. Season to taste with salt and pepper. (For a gas grill, preheat grill. Reduce heat to medium. Adjust for indirect cooking. Grill as above.)

Per serving: 136 cal., 6 g total fat (4 g sat. fat), 15 mg chol., 50 mg sodium, 19 g carbo., 2 g fiber, 3 g pro.
Daily Values: 5% vit. A, 31% vit. C, 2% calcium, 9% iron

Cheesy Peas and Potatoes

Jazzed-up with sizzling salami, this hash brown side dish is hearty enough to be a meal all by itself.

Prep: 15 minutes **Grill:** 17 minutes **Makes:** 4 side-dish servings

  4 ounces process cheese food with mild Mexican flavor

  ½ of a 16-ounce package (2 cups) frozen loose-pack hash brown potatoes
    with onions and peppers

  ¾ cup frozen peas

  ¼ cup chopped salami

1. Melt cheese food in a medium saucepan over low heat. Stir in the hash brown potatoes, peas, and salami.

2. Tear off a 36×18-inch piece of heavy foil; fold in half to make an 18-inch square. Place the potato mixture in center of the foil square. Bring up two opposite edges of foil; seal with a double fold. Fold remaining edges together to completely enclose potato mixture, leaving space for steam to build.

3. For a charcoal grill, grill foil packet on the rack of an uncovered grill directly over medium coals for 17 to 25 minutes or until heated through, turning packet once halfway through grilling. (For a gas grill, preheat grill. Reduce heat to medium. Place foil packet on grill rack over heat. Cover and grill as above.)

Per serving: 195 cal., 11 g total fat (6 g sat. fat), 34 mg chol., 841 mg sodium, 15 g carbo., 2 g fiber, 10 g pro.
Daily Values: 17% vit. A, 15% vit. C, 16% calcium, 5% iron

Foil Packet Grilling

One of the slickest ways to cook on the grill is to use aluminum foil packets. Here's how:

- Start with a large sheet of heavy foil—it's better to have too much than too little.

- If you think there's a chance the food might stick, use nonstick cooking spray on the inside of your packet.

- Place the food in the center of the sheet.

- Bring together two opposite sides of the foil, sealing them with a double fold. Leave a little extra space for steam to build.

- Seal the remaining sides with another double fold.

Peppered Steak Fries

Prep: 15 minutes **Cook:** 10 minutes **Grill:** 6 minutes **Makes:** 6 side-dish servings

    4 medium baking potatoes
    2 tablespoons cooking oil
    1 to 1¼ teaspoons cracked black pepper
    ½ teaspoon salt

1. Scrub potatoes and pat dry. Cut potatoes in half lengthwise; cut each half into 6 wedges. Cook potatoes, covered, in a small amount of boiling water about 10 minutes or until almost tender. Drain and cool. Put potato wedges in a large bowl.

2. Combine oil, pepper, and salt; drizzle over potatoes. Toss gently, being careful not to break the potato wedges.

3. For a charcoal grill, grill potato wedges on the rack of an uncovered grill directly over medium coals for 6 to 10 minutes or until brown, turning occasionally. (For a gas grill, preheat grill. Reduce heat to medium. Place potato wedges on grill rack over heat. Cover and grill as above.)

Per serving: 125 cal., 5 g total fat (1 g sat. fat), 0 mg chol., 202 mg sodium, 19 g carbo., 2 g fiber, 3 g pro.
Daily Values: 30% vit. C, 2% calcium, 9% iron

Potato Wedges with Orange Peel

Prep: 20 minutes **Cook:** 10 minutes **Grill:** 6 minutes **Makes:** 8 side-dish servings

> 4 large baking potatoes
>
> 4 large sweet potatoes
>
> 6 tablespoons olive oil
>
> 1 teaspoon salt
>
> ½ teaspoon ground pepper
>
> 2 teaspoons grated orange peel

1. Scrub potatoes and pat dry. Cut potatoes in half lengthwise; cut each half into 6 wedges. Cook potatoes, covered, in boiling water about 10 minutes or until almost tender. Drain and cool.

2. Transfer wedges to a large cookie sheet. Combine 4 tablespoons of the oil, salt, and pepper; brush over potatoes. Combine the remaining 2 tablespoons of oil and orange peel; set aside.

3. For a charcoal grill, grill potato wedges on the rack of an uncovered grill directly over medium coals for 6 to 10 minutes or until brown, turning occasionally. (For a gas grill, preheat grill. Reduce heat to medium. Place potato wedges on grill rack over heat. Cover and grill as above.)

4. To serve, transfer potato wedges to a serving plate; brush with orange peel mixture.

Per serving: 342 cal., 10 g total fat (1 g sat. fat), 0 mg chol., 394 mg sodium, 58 g carbo., 7 g fiber, 6 g pro.
Daily Values: 434% vit. A, 44% vit. C, 7% calcium, 17% iron

Fire-Roasted Acorn Squash

Prep: 10 minutes **Grill:** 45 minutes **Makes:** 4 side-dish servings

- 1 **tablespoon olive oil**
- ½ **teaspoon salt**
- ¼ **teaspoon black pepper**
- 2 **small acorn squash, cut crosswise into 1-inch rings and seeded**
- 2 **tablespoons butter or margarine, melted**
- 2 **teaspoons snipped fresh tarragon or ½ teaspoon dried tarragon, crushed**

1. In a small bowl combine oil, salt, and pepper; brush over squash rings. In another small bowl combine melted butter and tarragon. Set butter mixture aside.

2. For a charcoal grill, arrange medium-hot coals around a drip pan. Test for medium heat above the pan. Place squash rings on grill rack over drip pan. Cover and grill about 45 minutes or until squash is tender, turning squash occasionally and brushing with butter mixture during the last 15 minutes of grilling. (For a gas grill, preheat grill. Reduce heat to medium. Adjust for indirect cooking. Grill as above.)

Per serving: 153 cal., 10 g total fat (4 g sat. fat), 16 mg chol., 358 mg sodium, 18 g carbo., 3 g fiber, 1 g pro.
Daily Values: 16% vit. A, 27% vit. C, 6% calcium, 7% iron

Garlicky Grilled Portobellos

Portobellos are among nature's best vegetables for grilling. Heighten their meaty flavor with a butter and garlic brush-on.

Prep: 15 minutes **Grill:** 6 minutes **Makes:** 4 side-dish servings

        1 pound fresh portobello mushrooms
        ¼ cup butter or margarine, melted
        3 cloves garlic, minced
        ¼ teaspoon salt
        ⅛ teaspoon black pepper
        1 tablespoon snipped fresh chives

1. Wash mushrooms; remove and discard stems and gills.

2. In a bowl combine melted butter, garlic, salt, and pepper; brush over mushrooms.

3. For a charcoal grill, grill mushrooms on the rack of an uncovered grill directly over medium coals for 6 to 8 minutes or just until mushrooms are tender, turning once halfway through grilling. (For a gas grill, preheat grill. Reduce heat to medium. Place mushrooms on grill rack over heat. Cover and grill as above.)

4. To serve, sprinkle mushrooms with chives.

Per serving: 146 cal., 12 g total fat (7 g sat. fat), 31 mg chol., 241 mg sodium, 6 g carbo., 4 g fiber, 4 g pro.
Daily Values: 8% vit. A, 2% vit. C, 6% calcium, 3% iron

Smoked Mushrooms

Prep: 10 minutes **Soak:** 1 hour **Grill:** 45 minutes **Makes:** 4 to 6 side-dish servings

- 2 cups hickory wood chips
- 4 cups halved fresh mushrooms
- ¼ cup butter or margarine, cut up
- 1 teaspoon instant chicken bouillon granules

1. At least 1 hour before grilling, soak wood chips in water.

2. Combine mushrooms, butter, and bouillon granules in a disposable foil pan.

3. Drain wood chips. For a charcoal grill, arrange medium-hot coals around edge of grill. Sprinkle wood chips over coals. Test for medium heat above center of grill. Place the foil pan on grill rack over center of grill. Cover and grill for 45 to 60 minutes, stirring occasionally. (For a gas grill, preheat grill. Reduce heat to medium. Adjust for indirect cooking. Grill as above.)

Per serving: 130 cal., 13 g total fat (8 g sat. fat), 31 mg chol., 306 mg sodium, 3 g carbo., 1 g fiber, 3 g pro.
Daily Values: 7% vit. A, 1% calcium, 3% iron

Herb-Grilled Tomatoes

The creamy tartness of sour cream, combined with the herbal zing of basil, brings out the best in tomatoes' signature summertime flavor. See photo on page 167.

Prep: 15 minutes **Grill:** 10 minutes **Makes:** 4 side-dish servings

- 4 small tomatoes, cored and halved crosswise
- 3 tablespoons dairy sour cream or plain yogurt
- 1 tablespoon snipped fresh basil or 1 teaspoon dried basil, crushed
- 1 tablespoon fine dry bread crumbs
- 1 tablespoon finely shredded Parmesan cheese

1. Spread cut sides of tomatoes with sour cream. Arrange tomatoes in a disposable foil pie pan. In a small bowl combine basil, bread crumbs, and Parmesan cheese; sprinkle evenly over tomato halves.

2. For a charcoal grill, arrange medium-hot coals around edge of grill. Test for medium heat above center of grill. Place foil pan on grill rack over center of grill. Cover and grill for 10 to 15 minutes or until heated through. (For a gas grill, preheat grill. Reduce heat to medium. Adjust for indirect cooking. Grill as above.)

Per serving: 81 cal., 4 g total fat (3 g sat. fat), 10 mg chol., 197 mg sodium, 6 g carbo., 1 g fiber, 5 g pro.
Daily Values: 22% vit. A, 24% vit. C, 13% calcium, 3% iron

Grilled Sweet Onions

The perfect complement to grilled steak, sweet onions such as Walla Walla, Vidalia, and Maui take on added richness when kissed by the flame.

Prep: 15 minutes **Grill:** 35 minutes **Makes:** 4 side-dish servings

- 4 medium sweet onions (4 to 5 ounces each)
- 1 tablespoon butter or margarine, melted
- 1 teaspoon Dijon-style mustard
- ⅛ teaspoon bottled hot pepper sauce
- 1 tablespoon brown sugar
- Black pepper

1. Peel onions; cut almost through each onion forming 8 wedges. Tear off four 12-inch squares of heavy foil. Place an onion in the center of each foil square. Combine butter, mustard, and hot pepper sauce; drizzle over onions. Sprinkle with brown sugar. Bring up two opposite edges of foil and seal with a double fold. Fold remaining edges together to completely enclose each onion, leaving space for steam to build.

2. For a charcoal grill, arrange medium-hot coals around drip pan. Test for medium heat above pan. Place foil packets on grill rack over drip pan. Cover and grill about 25 minutes or until onions are nearly tender. Cut a 2-inch opening in the top of each foil packet. Cover and grill about 10 minutes more or until the onions are lightly brown. Sprinkle with the pepper. (For a gas grill, preheat grill. Reduce heat to medium. Adjust for indirect cooking. Grill as above.)

Per serving: 83 cal., 3 g total fat (1 g sat. fat), 0 mg chol., 70 mg sodium, 13 g carbo., 2 g fiber, 1 g pro.
Daily Values: 3% vit. A, 8% vit. C, 2% calcium, 2% iron

Sweet Onions

Few vegetables can match the visual and flavor appeal of grilled sweet onions served alongside a sizzling grilled entrée. With their slightly flattened appearance and light, papery skins, sweet onions are a breed apart from more common yellow, white, and red varieties. Top sweet onion varieties to look for are Vidalia, Maui, Walla Walla, and the South American overachiever Oso Sweet, which sometimes features twice the sweetness of delectable Vidalias.

Summer Green Beans

After grilling, mash the pulp from the garlic cloves into a delicious paste to blend into the cooked beans.

Prep: 20 minutes **Grill:** 25 minutes **Makes:** 4 side-dish servings

12 ounces green beans, trimmed

8 cloves garlic, unpeeled

1 tablespoon water

1 teaspoon cooking oil

1 or 2 fresh jalapeño chile peppers, cut into thin strips (do not seed) (see tip, page 34)

2 teaspoons lemon-flavored olive oil

Salt

1. In a large bowl toss together beans, garlic, water, cooking oil, and chile pepper; set aside. Tear off a 36×18-inch piece of heavy foil; fold in half to make an 18-inch square. Place bean mixture in center of foil square. Bring up two opposite edges of foil and seal with a double fold. Fold remaining edges together to completely enclose beans, leaving space for steam to build.

2. For a charcoal grill, grill foil packet on the rack of an uncovered grill directly over medium coals for 20 minutes, turning packet once. Remove packet from grill; cool slightly. Carefully open packet; return open packet to grill rack. Continue grilling about 5 minutes more or until the beans are crisp-tender, stirring occasionally. (For a gas grill, preheat grill. Reduce heat to medium. Place foil packet on grill rack over heat. Cover and grill as above.)

3. To serve, transfer beans to a serving bowl; drizzle with olive oil. Remove peel from garlic cloves; mash lightly and stir into beans. Season to taste with salt.

Per serving: 59 cal., 4 g total fat (0 g sat. fat), 0 mg chol., 78 mg sodium, 7 g carbo., 3 g fiber, 2 g pro.
Daily Values: 10% vit. A, 21% vit. C, 3% calcium, 5% iron

Picante Avocados

Avocado halves make a splendid side dish when grilled and filled with a zesty blend of picante sauce and cheese.

Prep: 10 minutes **Grill:** 10 minutes **Makes:** 4 side-dish servings

- 1 tablespoon olive oil
- 1 tablespoon lime juice
- 2 large ripe avocados, halved, seeded, and peeled
- ⅛ teaspoon salt
- ¼ cup bottled picante sauce
- ¼ cup shredded Monterey Jack cheese
- Snipped fresh cilantro (optional)
- Salad greens (optional)
- Bottled picante sauce (optional)
- Dairy sour cream (optional)

1. Combine olive oil and lime juice; brush over all sides of both avocados. Sprinkle cut sides of avocados with salt.

2. For a charcoal grill, grill avocado halves, cut sides down, on the rack of an uncovered grill directly over medium coals about 5 minutes or until brown. Turn avocado halves cut sides up. Fill centers of avocado halves with the ¼ cup picante sauce and shredded cheese. Cover and grill about 5 minutes more or until cheese begins to melt. (For a gas grill, preheat grill. Reduce heat to medium. Place avocado halves on grill rack over heat. Cover and grill as above.)

3. Remove avocados from grill. If desired, sprinkle tops with cilantro and serve on a bed of salad greens with additional picante sauce and sour cream.

Per serving: 204 cal., 19 g total fat (4 g sat. fat), 6 mg chol., 292 mg sodium, 9 g carbo., 6 g fiber, 4 g pro.
Daily Values: 6% vit. A, 15% vit. C, 7% calcium, 4% iron

Herbed Sweet Corn

Prep: 20 minutes **Grill:** 25 minutes **Makes:** 6 side-dish servings

⅓ cup butter, softened

3 tablespoons snipped fresh chives, parsley, cilantro, or tarragon

¼ teaspoon salt

¼ teaspoon black pepper

6 fresh ears sweet corn with husks

1. In a small bowl combine butter, chives, salt, and pepper. Set butter mixture aside.

2. Carefully peel back corn husks but do not remove. Remove and discard the silk. Gently rinse corn; pat dry. Spread about 1 tablespoon of the butter mixture over each ear of corn. Carefully fold husks back around ears. Tie husk tops with 100-percent-cotton kitchen string to secure.

3. For a charcoal grill, grill corn on the rack of an uncovered grill directly over medium coals for 25 to 30 minutes or until kernels are tender, turning and rearranging ears 3 times using long-handle tongs. (For a gas grill, preheat grill. Reduce heat to medium. Place corn on grill rack over heat. Cover and grill as above.)

4. Remove string from corn. Remove the husks. If desired, serve with any remaining butter mixture.

Per serving: 168 cal., 11 g total fat (7 g sat. fat), 27 mg chol., 182 mg sodium, 17 g carbo., 2 g fiber, 3 g pro.
Daily Values: 11% vit. A, 12% vit. C, 1% calcium, 3% iron

Corn and Tomato Salad

See photo on page 168.

Prep: 20 minutes **Grill:** 25 minutes **Stand:** 20 minutes **Makes:** 6 side-dish servings

    6 fresh ears sweet corn with husks
    ½ of an 8-ounce bottle Italian salad dressing
    3 tablespoons snipped fresh rosemary
    3 to 6 cups fresh baby spinach leaves or spinach leaves
    4 medium roma tomatoes, finely chopped

1. Carefully peel back corn husks but do not remove. Remove and discard the silk. Gently rinse corn; pat dry. Brush each ear of corn with a little of the salad dressing; sprinkle each ear with some of the rosemary. Carefully fold husks back around ears. Tie husk tops with 100-percent-cotton kitchen string to secure.

2. For a charcoal grill, grill corn on the rack of an uncovered grill directly over medium coals for 25 to 30 minutes or until kernels are tender, turning and rearranging ears 3 times using long-handle tongs. (For a gas grill, preheat grill. Reduce heat to medium. Place corn on grill rack over heat. Cover and grill as above.)

3. Remove string from corn. Remove the husks; cool slightly. When cool enough to handle, use a sharp knife to cut the corn kernels off the cobs. For dressing, in a small bowl combine the remaining salad dressing and rosemary.

4. To serve, arrange spinach on 6 salad plates; top with corn kernels and tomatoes. Serve with dressing.

Per serving: 138 cal., 3 g total fat (0 g sat. fat), 1 mg chol., 414 mg sodium, 28 g carbo., 5 g fiber, 4 g pro.
Daily Values: 27% vit. A, 29% vit. C, 2% calcium, 11% iron

Asparagus in Dill Butter

As one of spring's earliest and most delicious arrivals, fresh asparagus is a great way to kick off the grilling season.

Prep: 10 minutes **Grill:** 7 minutes **Makes:** 4 to 6 side-dish servings

- 1 pound asparagus spears, trimmed
- 2 tablespoons butter or margarine, melted
- 1 tablespoon snipped fresh dill or 1 teaspoon dried dill
- 1 clove garlic, minced
- ¼ teaspoon black pepper
  Finely shredded Parmesan cheese

1. Place asparagus in a disposable foil pan. Drizzle with butter; sprinkle with dill, garlic, and pepper. Toss to combine.

2. For a charcoal grill, grill foil pan on the rack of an uncovered grill directly over medium coals for 7 to 10 minutes or until asparagus is crisp-tender, stirring occasionally. (For a gas grill, preheat grill. Reduce heat to medium. Place foil pan on grill rack over heat. Cover and grill as above.)

3. To serve, transfer asparagus to a serving dish. Sprinkle with Parmesan cheese.

Per serving: 142 cal., 11 g total fat (7 g sat. fat), 28 mg chol., 355 mg sodium, 2 g carbo., 1 g fiber, 8 g pro.
Daily Values: 9% vit. A, 27% vit. C, 22% calcium, 4% iron

Asparagus with Cheese and Chives

Prep: 25 minutes **Cook:** 2 minutes **Grill:** 2 minutes **Makes:** 6 to 8 side-dish servings

    2 pounds asparagus spears, trimmed
    2 tablespoons olive oil
       Salt and black pepper
    2 ounces Parmesan cheese, shaved
    1 tablespoon snipped fresh chives

1. Divide asparagus into four equal portions; tie portions into bundles with 100-percent-cotton kitchen string.

2. Fill a 4-quart Dutch oven halfway with lightly salted water. Bring to boiling; add asparagus bundles. Return to boiling. Cook, uncovered, for 2 minutes. Immediately plunge asparagus bundles into a bowl of ice water; drain.

3. Untie bundles and spread asparagus on a cookie sheet. Drizzle 1 tablespoon of the olive oil over the asparagus; sprinkle with salt and pepper.

4. For a charcoal grill, grill asparagus on the rack of an uncovered grill directly over medium coals for 2 to 3 minutes or until crisp-tender, turning occasionally. (For a gas grill, preheat grill. Reduce heat to medium. Place asparagus on grill rack over heat. Cover and grill as above.)

5. To serve, transfer asparagus to a serving dish. Drizzle with the remaining 1 tablespoon olive oil; sprinkle with cheese and chives.

Per serving: 95 cal., 7 g total fat (2 g sat. fat), 7 mg chol., 259 mg sodium, 3 g carbo., 2 g fiber, 5 g pro.
Daily Values: 13% vit. A, 7% vit. C, 14% calcium, 10% iron

Italian Breadsticks

Cooking breadsticks directly over the flame imparts a rustic flavor similar to brick-oven baking. See photo on page 169.

Prep: 10 minutes **Grill:** 2 minutes **Makes:** 8 breadsticks

½ cup grated Parmesan cheese

1¼ teaspoons dried Italian seasoning, crushed

¼ teaspoon crushed red pepper

8 purchased soft breadsticks

3 tablespoons butter or margarine, melted

1. In a shallow dish combine Parmesan cheese, Italian seasoning, and crushed red pepper. Brush each breadstick with melted butter; roll in Parmesan cheese mixture to coat.

2. For a charcoal grill, grill breadsticks on the rack of an uncovered grill directly over medium coals for 2 to 3 minutes or until golden, turning to brown evenly. Serve warm. (For a gas grill, preheat grill. Reduce heat to medium. Place breadsticks on grill rack over heat. Cover and grill as above.)

Per breadstick: 194 cal., 7 g total fat (4 g sat. fat), 16 mg chol., 430 mg sodium, 25 g carbo., 1 g fiber, 7 g pro.
Daily Values: 4% vit. A, 15% calcium, 11% iron

Grilled French Bread

Prep: 10 minutes **Grill:** 3 minutes **Makes:** 8 to 10 side-dish servings

- ¼ cup butter
- ¼ cup grated Parmesan cheese
- 2 tablespoons snipped fresh parsley
- 1 clove garlic, minced
- ⅛ teaspoon cayenne pepper (optional)
- 1 16-ounce loaf unsliced French bread

1. In a medium skillet melt butter; stir in Parmesan cheese, parsley, garlic, and, if desired, cayenne pepper. Set butter mixture aside.

2. Cut French bread in half lengthwise. For a charcoal grill, grill bread, cut sides down, on the rack of an uncovered grill directly over medium coals about 2 minutes or until toasted. Turn cut sides up; brush with butter mixture. Grill for 1 to 2 minutes more. (For a gas grill, preheat grill. Reduce heat to medium. Place bread on grill rack over heat. Cover and grill as above.)

3. To serve, cut into 2-inch slices.

Per serving: 169 cal., 3 g total fat (1 g sat. fat), 3 mg chol., 385 mg sodium, 30 g carbo., 2 g fiber, 6 g pro.
Daily Values: 2% vit. A, 2% vit. C, 7% calcium, 9% iron

Toasty-Hot French Bread Slices

Watching this mixture of butter, honey, and sage oozing into fire-toasted French bread slices is almost as good as the eating—but not quite!

Prep: 20 minutes **Grill:** 2 minutes **Makes:** 6 side-dish servings

   2 tablespoons creamy Dijon-style mustard blend

   1 tablespoon butter or margarine, melted

   1 teaspoon honey

   ½ teaspoon dried sage, crushed

   ⅛ teaspoon black pepper

   6 1-inch slices French or Italian bread

1. Combine mustard blend, butter, honey, sage, and pepper. Set mustard mixture aside.

2. For a charcoal grill, grill bread slices on the rack of an uncovered grill directly over medium coals for 1 to 2 minutes or until bottoms are toasted. Turn bread over. Carefully spread the toasted sides with mustard mixture. Grill for 1 to 2 minutes more or until bottoms are toasted. (For a gas grill, preheat grill. Reduce heat to medium. Place bread slices on grill rack over heat. Cover and grill as above.)

Per serving: 164 cal., 4 g total fat (1 g sat. fat), 5 mg chol., 389 mg sodium, 28 g carbo., 2 g fiber, 4 g pro.
Daily Values: 1% vit. A, 4% calcium, 7% iron

Herbed Baguette

Prep: 10 minutes **Grill:** 2 minutes **Makes:** 8 side-dish servings

- 1 8-ounce loaf baguette-style French bread
- 2 tablespoons olive oil
- 1 tablespoon snipped fresh parsley and/or chives

1. Cut bread into 16 slices. Combine oil and parsley; brush one side of each bread slice with some of the oil mixture.

2. For a charcoal grill, grill the bread slices on the rack of an uncovered grill directly over medium coals for 2 to 4 minutes or until toasted, turning once. (For a gas grill, preheat grill. Reduce heat to medium. Place the bread slices on grill rack over heat. Cover and grill as above.)

Per serving: 108 cal., 4 g total fat (1 g sat. fat), 0 mg chol., 173 mg sodium, 15 g carbo., 1 g fiber, 3 g pro.
Daily Values: 1% vit. A, 1% vit. C, 2% calcium, 4% iron

Gas Grill Features

There's no denying it: Gas grills are extraordinarily convenient. For most models, all you have to do is turn a valve, push a button, and within minutes you're off and grilling.

When purchasing a gas grill, look for multiple burners with individual control over each burner. This feature enables indirect grilling or barbecuing in addition to direct grilling over the flames. And when purchasing any type of grill, remember that solid construction is a virtue all its own.

Fill-the-Grill Nectarine Toss

Not only is this a beautifully simple dessert, you could skip the ice cream and serve the nectarines as a side dish alongside grilled pork. See photo on page 170.

Prep: 15 minutes **Grill:** 8 minutes **Makes:** 6 servings

6 ripe medium nectarines, halved and pitted

2 tablespoons olive oil

Ground cinnamon or nutmeg (optional)

3 cups vanilla ice cream

Coarsely chopped chocolate chunks

1. Brush nectarines with olive oil. If desired, sprinkle with cinnamon. For a charcoal grill, place a grill wok or grill basket on the rack of an uncovered grill directly over medium coals; heat for 5 minutes. Place nectarine halves in the wok or basket. Grill for 8 to 10 minutes or until heated through, turning gently halfway through grilling. (For gas grill, preheat grill. Reduce heat to medium. Place grill wok or grill basket on grill rack over heat. Cover and grill as above.)

2. To serve, place ice cream in a large serving bowl. Top with grilled nectarine halves. Sprinkle with chocolate chunks.

Per serving: 312 cal., 19 g total fat (9 g sat. fat), 46 mg chol., 46 mg sodium, 36 g carbo., 2 g fiber, 4 g pro.
Daily Values: 13% vit. C, 10% calcium, 1% iron

Banana Split Kabobs

See photo on page 170.

Prep: 20 minutes **Grill:** 5 minutes **Makes:** 4 servings

    3   medium bananas, cut into 1-inch chunks
    1½ cups large strawberries, halved
    1½ cups fresh pineapple chunks
    1   pint vanilla ice cream
    ½   cup caramel and/or chocolate ice cream topping
        Chopped nuts (optional)
        Whipped cream (optional)
        Maraschino cherries (optional)

1. On eight 6- to 8-inch metal skewers, alternately thread bananas, strawberries, and pineapple, leaving a ¼-inch space between pieces.

2. For a charcoal grill, grill kabobs on the rack of an uncovered grill directly over medium coals about 5 minutes or until fruits are warm and bananas are lightly brown, turning occasionally. (For a gas grill, preheat grill. Reduce heat to medium. Place kabobs on grill rack over heat. Cover and grill as above.)

3. To serve, place a scoop of ice cream and 2 fruit skewers in each serving dish. Drizzle with caramel and/or chocolate ice cream topping and, if desired, sprinkle with nuts. If desired, garnish each serving with whipped cream and cherries.

Per serving: 434 cal., 13 g total fat (8 g sat. fat), 45 mg chol., 153 mg sodium, 79 g carbo., 5 g fiber, 4 g pro.
Daily Values: 15% vit. A, 80% vit. C, 13% calcium, 4% iron

Honey-Glazed Bananas

If substituting plantains for bananas, use fruit with dark or black peels—they're at their ripest.

Prep: 5 minutes **Grill:** 4 minutes **Makes:** 4 servings

  2 tablespoons butter, melted
  1 tablespoon honey
  1 teaspoon vinegar
  ⅛ teaspoon cayenne pepper
  2 large ripe bananas or plantains, peeled and halved lengthwise
     Vanilla ice cream or pound cake (optional)

1. In a small bowl combine butter, honey, vinegar, and cayenne pepper; brush generously over bananas.

2. For a charcoal grill, grill bananas on the rack of an uncovered grill directly over medium coals about 4 minutes or until brown and heated through, turning once and brushing with the remaining honey mixture halfway through grilling. (For a gas grill, preheat grill. Reduce heat to medium. Place bananas on grill rack over heat. Cover and grill as above.)

3. If desired, serve over ice cream.

Per serving: 133 cal., 6 g total fat (1 g sat. fat), 0 mg chol., 68 mg sodium, 21 g carbo., 1 g fiber, 1 g pro.
Daily Values: 10% vit. C, 1% iron

Peaches with Quick Cherry Sauce

Prep: 15 minutes **Grill:** 6 minutes **Makes:** 6 servings

      3 medium peaches or nectarines, pitted and quartered
      3 tablespoons orange juice
   1½ cups fresh or frozen unsweetened pitted dark sweet cherries, thawed
      ½ cup cherry jam
      3 cups vanilla ice cream
      2 tablespoons coconut or almonds, toasted (optional)

1. Brush each peach with 1 tablespoon of the orange juice. Thread peaches onto 2 long metal skewers, leaving a 1¼-inch space between pieces. Set aside.

2. For sauce, in a small saucepan combine the remaining orange juice, cherries, and cherry jam. Bring to boiling over medium heat, stirring frequently; reduce heat. Simmer, uncovered, for 3 minutes. Set sauce aside.

3. For a charcoal grill, grill skewers on the rack of an uncovered grill directly over medium coals for 6 to 8 minutes or until heated through, turning once halfway through grilling. (For a gas grill, preheat grill. Reduce heat to medium. Place skewers on grill rack over heat. Cover and grill as above.)

4. To serve, spoon peaches over scoops of ice cream; top with sauce. If desired, sprinkle with coconut.

Per serving: 304 cal., 12 g total fat (7 g sat. fat), 68 mg chol., 54 mg sodium, 46 g carbo., 2 g fiber, 4 g pro.
Daily Values: 14% vit. A, 20% vit. C, 10% calcium, 4% iron

Peanut Butter S'mores

Prep: 15 minutes **Grill:** 7 minutes **Makes:** 8 servings

> ¾ cup peanut butter
> 4 9- to 10-inch flour tortillas
> 1 cup tiny marshmallows
> ½ cup miniature semisweet chocolate pieces
> 1 medium ripe banana, thinly sliced

1. Spread about 3 tablespoons of the peanut butter over one half of each tortilla. Top each with some of the marshmallows, chocolate pieces, and banana slices. Fold tortillas in half, pressing gently to flatten and seal slightly.

2. For a charcoal grill, grill filled tortillas on the rack of an uncovered grill directly over medium coals for 7 to 9 minutes or until tortillas are golden and chocolate is melted, turning once halfway through grilling. (For a gas grill, preheat grill. Reduce heat to medium. Place filled tortillas on grill rack over heat. Cover and grill as above.)

3. To serve, cut each filled tortilla into 4 wedges.

Per serving: 288 cal., 17 g total fat (4 g sat. fat), 0 mg chol., 206 mg sodium, 32 g carbo., 3 g fiber, 9 g pro.
Daily Values: 2% vit. C, 4% calcium, 8% iron

Pear Tart

A treat for the senses, this grilled pear tart combines smoky-spicy fragrance, luxurious fruit flavor, and old-world visual charm.

Prep: 20 minutes **Grill:** 35 minutes **Cool:** 20 minutes **Makes:** 6 to 8 servings

- ½ of a 15-ounce package rolled refrigerated unbaked piecrust (1 crust)
- 2 large ripe pears, peeled, cored, and very thinly sliced (3½ cups)
- 2 tablespoons sugar
- 1 tablespoon cornstarch
- ¼ teaspoon ground cardamom
- Whipped cream (optional)

1. Let piecrust stand according to package directions. Meanwhile, in a medium bowl, toss pear slices with sugar, cornstarch, and cardamom. Wrap a 10- to 12-inch pizza pan with heavy foil.

2. Unroll piecrust on the pizza pan. Arrange pear slices in center of piecrust in a single layer, leaving a 2-inch border around the edge. Fold piecrust border up over the pears, pleating as necessary to fit.

3. For a charcoal grill, arrange medium-hot coals around edge of grill. Test for medium heat above center of grill. Place pizza pan on grill rack over center of grill. Cover and grill for 35 to 45 minutes or until pears are tender and pastry is golden brown. (For a gas grill, preheat grill. Reduce heat to medium. Adjust for indirect cooking. Grill as above.)

4. Let tart cool on a wire rack for 20 to 30 minutes before serving. If desired, serve with whipped cream.

Per serving: 234 cal., 9 g total fat (4 g sat. fat), 7 mg chol., 145 mg sodium, 37 g carbo., 3 g fiber, 1 g pro.
Daily Values: 7% vit. C, 1% calcium, 1% iron

Pineapple Fries with Raspberry Ketchup

See photo on page 171.

Prep: 20 minutes **Grill:** 5 minutes **Makes:** 6 servings

- 1 medium fresh pineapple
- 2 cups loose-pack frozen raspberries, thawed
- 1 to 2 tablespoons sugar
  Nonstick cooking spray
- 6 large waffle cones

1. Remove the crown and cut off the top and base of the pineapple. Cut off wide strips of peel. Remove the eyes by cutting narrow wedge-shape grooves diagonally around fruit, following the pattern of the eyes. Slice pineapple lengthwise into ½-inch-thick slices. Coarsely chop ⅓ cup of the pineapple from an end piece. Set remaining slices aside.

2. For ketchup, in a blender combine the thawed raspberries and sugar. Cover and blend until smooth. Press berry mixture through a sieve or strainer; discard seeds. Return sieved berry mixture to blender; add the ⅓ cup chopped pineapple. Cover and blend until smooth. Cover and chill ketchup until serving time.

3. Lightly coat pineapple slices with nonstick cooking spray. For a charcoal grill, grill pineapple slices on the rack of an uncovered grill directly over hot coals for 5 to 7 minutes, turning once halfway through grilling. (For a gas grill, preheat grill. Place pineapple slices on grill rack over high heat. Cover and grill as above.)

4. Remove pineapple slices from grill; cool slightly. Cut grilled pineapple into strips about ½ inch wide. Divide pineapple fries among waffle cones; top with some of the ketchup. Pass remaining ketchup.

Per serving: 158 cal., 1 g total fat (0 g sat. fat), 0 mg chol., 36 mg sodium, 35 g carbo., 5 g fiber, 2 g pro.
Daily Values: 2% vit. A, 43% vit. C, 3% calcium, 9% iron

Gorgonzola-Walnut-Stuffed Apples

There's no place like the grill for melding classic, sophisticated flavor pairings such as these. See photo on page 171.

Prep: 20 minutes **Grill:** 30 minutes **Makes:** 4 servings

  4 medium cooking apples (such as Granny Smith or Jonathan)

  ¼ cup crumbled Gorgonzola, Stilton, or Roquefort cheese

  ¼ cup chopped walnuts

  2 tablespoons butter or margarine, melted

  4 teaspoons honey

     Honey (optional)

1. Core apples almost to the bottom, leaving approximately ½ inch. Remove 1 inch of peel from the top of each apple.

2. In a small bowl combine Gorgonzola cheese, walnuts, and melted butter. Fill each cored apple three-fourths full of the cheese mixture. Drizzle 1 teaspoon honey into each. Add the remaining cheese mixture to apples. Place apples in a disposable foil pan.

3. For a charcoal grill, arrange medium-hot coals around edge of grill. Test for medium heat above center of grill. Place foil pan on grill rack over center of grill. Cover and grill for 30 to 40 minutes or until tender. (For a gas grill, preheat grill. Reduce heat to medium. Adjust for indirect cooking. Grill as above.)

4. If desired, drizzle each serving with additional honey; serve warm.

Per serving: 218 cal., 13 g total fat (5 g sat. fat), 21 mg chol., 142 mg sodium, 26 g carbo., 4 g fiber, 3 g pro.
Daily Values: 6% vit. A, 11% vit. C, 6% calcium, 2% iron

Dessert Burritos

See photo on page 172.

Prep: 10 minutes **Grill:** 13 minutes **Cool:** 5 minutes **Makes:** 4 servings

- 4 9- to 10-inch flour tortillas
- ¼ cup caramel ice cream topping
- 1 medium ripe banana, sliced
- ½ cup crushed chocolate sandwich cookies with white filling
- 2 tablespoons butter, melted

Desired flavor of jam and/or whipped cream (optional)

1. Wrap tortillas in foil. For a charcoal grill, grill tortilla packet on the rack of an uncovered grill directly over medium coals about 10 minutes or until warm, turning once halfway through grilling. Spread 1 tablespoon ice cream topping down the center of each tortilla. Top with 3 or 4 banana slices and 2 tablespoons crushed cookies. Fold one-third of the tortilla over filling. Fold in ends and roll up, forming a burrito. Secure with wooden toothpicks. Brush with melted butter.

2. Grill burritos directly over medium heat for 3 to 4 minutes or until tortillas are lightly browned, turning once halfway through grilling. (For a gas grill, preheat grill. Reduce heat to medium. Place tortilla packet and burritos on grill rack over heat. Cover and grill as above.)

3. Remove burritos from grill; let cool 5 minutes. If desired, serve with jam and/or whipped cream.

Per serving: 358 cal., 13 g total fat (5 g sat. fat), 16 mg chol., 382 mg sodium, 56 g carbo., 3 g fiber, 4 g pro.
Daily Values: 4% vit. A, 4% vit. C, 6% calcium, 12% iron

quick serve-alongs

Saucepan Baked Beans

Up against the clock? No worries—this blazing-fast baked bean side dish is whipped together in a jiffy.

Prep: 10 minutes **Cook:** 10 minutes **Makes:** 6 side-dish servings

- 1 16-ounce can pork and beans in tomato sauce
- 1 15-ounce can navy or Great Northern beans, rinsed and drained
- ¼ cup ketchup
- 2 tablespoons maple-flavored syrup or brown sugar
- 2 teaspoons dry mustard
- ¼ cup cooked bacon pieces

1. In a medium saucepan combine pork and beans, navy beans, ketchup, syrup, and mustard. Bring to boiling; reduce heat. Simmer, uncovered, about 10 minutes or until desired consistency, stirring frequently. Stir in bacon pieces.

Per serving: 202 cal., 2 g total fat (1 g sat. fat), 8 mg chol., 846 mg sodium, 37 g carbo., 7 g fiber, 11 g pro.
Daily Values: 3% vit. A, 7% vit. C, 9% calcium, 23% iron

Beer-Simmered Beans

Prep: 10 minutes **Cook:** 10 minutes **Makes:** 7 side-dish servings

    1 15-ounce can pinto beans, drained and rinsed
    1 15-ounce can kidney beans, drained and rinsed
    1 cup light beer
    2 small jalapeño chile peppers, finely chopped (optional) (see tip, page 34)
    2 cloves garlic, minced
    1½ teaspoons ground cumin
    ¼ teaspoon salt

1. In a large saucepan combine pinto beans, kidney beans, beer, chile peppers (if desired), garlic, cumin, and salt. Bring to boiling; reduce heat. Simmer, covered, about 10 minutes or until desired consistency, stirring frequently.

Per serving: 113 cal., 0 g total fat (0 g sat. fat), 0 mg chol., 380 mg sodium, 21 g carbo., 7 g fiber, 8 g pro.
Daily Values: 4% calcium, 8% iron

Farm-Style Green Beans

Here's a tasty way to showcase summer's best veggies, fresh from the garden or farmer's market.

Prep: 20 minutes **Cook:** 10 minutes **Makes:** 8 side-dish servings

> 1 pound green beans, trimmed
>
> 4 slices bacon, cut up
>
> 2 medium onions, sliced
>
> 2 cups chopped, seeded, peeled tomato (3 medium)
>
> ½ teaspoon salt

1. Leave green beans whole or cut into 1-inch pieces; set aside.

2. In a large skillet cook bacon until crisp. Remove bacon, reserving 3 tablespoons drippings. Drain bacon on paper towels; set aside. Cook onion in the reserved drippings over medium heat until tender. Stir in tomato and salt. Cook, uncovered, about 5 minutes more or until most of the liquid is absorbed.

3. Meanwhile, in a medium saucepan cook green beans in a small amount of boiling salted water for 10 to 15 minutes or until crisp-tender; drain. Transfer beans to a serving bowl. Top beans with the tomato mixture and bacon.

Per serving: 99 cal., 7 g total fat (2 g sat. fat), 9 mg chol., 244 mg sodium, 8 g carbo., 3 g fiber, 3 g pro.
Daily Values: 14% vit. A, 24% vit. C, 3% calcium, 4% iron

Ranch Fries

Prep: 25 minutes **Bake:** 40 minutes **Oven:** 400°F **Makes:** 6 side-dish servings

Nonstick cooking spray
3 pounds potatoes, cut into 2×¼-inch pieces
1 2-ounce envelope dry ranch salad dressing mix

1. Lightly coat 2 cookie sheets with cooking spray; set aside.

2. In a large bowl combine the potatoes and salad dressing mix. Spread half of the potatoes in a single layer on each prepared cookie sheet; lightly coat potatoes with cooking spray.

3. Bake in a 400°F oven for 20 minutes; toss potatoes. Lightly coat potatoes again with cooking spray. Switch positions of cookie sheets in oven and bake about 20 minutes more or until potatoes are golden brown and crisp.

Per serving: 191 cal., 0 g total fat (0 g sat. fat), 0 mg chol., 678 mg sodium, 42 g carbo., 4 g fiber, 5 g pro.
Daily Values: 51% vit. C, 3% calcium, 17% iron

Easy Roasted Potatoes

Prep: 10 minutes **Bake:** 55 minutes **Oven:** 325°F **Makes:** 4 side-dish servings

  3 medium round red or white potatoes, cut into eighths, or 10 to 12 tiny new potatoes, halved
  2 tablespoons olive oil
  ½ teaspoon onion powder
  ¼ teaspoon salt
  ¼ teaspoon black pepper
  ⅛ teaspoon paprika
  1 clove garlic, minced

1. Place potatoes in a greased 9×9×2-inch baking pan. In a small bowl combine oil, onion powder, salt, pepper, paprika, and garlic. Drizzle oil mixture over potatoes; toss to coat.

2. Roast, uncovered, in a 325°F oven for 45 minutes. Stir potatoes; bake for 10 to 20 minutes more or until potatoes are tender and brown on the edges.

Per serving: 146 cal., 7 g total fat (1 g sat. fat), 0 mg chol., 154 mg sodium, 19 g carbo., 2 g fiber, 3 g pro.
Daily Values: 1% vit. A, 28% vit. C, 2% calcium, 9% iron

Cheesy Garlic Potato Gratin

Inspired by the French potato dish Gratin Dauphinois, this version is magnificent served alongside grilled entrées.

Prep: 15 minutes **Bake:** 1¼ hours **Oven:** 350°F **Makes:** 6 to 8 side-dish servings

1½ pounds Yukon gold or other yellow potatoes, thinly sliced (about 5 cups)
⅓ cup sliced green onion
1½ cups shredded Swiss cheese
4 cloves garlic, minced
1 teaspoon salt
¼ teaspoon black pepper
1 cup whipping cream

1. Grease a 2-quart square baking dish. Layer half of the sliced potatoes and half of the green onion in the dish. Sprinkle with half of the Swiss cheese, garlic, salt, and pepper. Repeat layers. Pour whipping cream over the top.

2. Bake, covered, in a 350°F oven for 1 hour. Uncover and bake for 15 to 20 minutes more or until potatoes are tender and top is golden brown.

Per serving: 365 cal., 23 g total fat (14 g sat. fat), 80 mg chol., 454 mg sodium, 30 g carbo., 1 g fiber, 12 g pro.
Daily Values: 25% vit. A, 31% vit. C, 26% calcium, 10% iron

Dilled Peas and Walnuts

A sprinkling of walnuts imparts a uniquely scrumptious flavor contrast to the sweetness of fresh peas.

Prep: 35 minutes **Makes:** 4 side-dish servings

    2 cups shelled peas or one 10-ounce package frozen peas
    ¼ cup chopped onion
    1 tablespoon butter or margarine
    1½ teaspoons snipped fresh dill or ½ teaspoon dried dill
    ¼ teaspoon salt
    ¼ teaspoon black pepper
    3 tablespoons broken walnuts or slivered almonds, toasted

1. Cook fresh peas and onion, covered, in a small amount of boiling salted water for 10 to 12 minutes or until crisp-tender. (Or cook frozen peas and onion according to the peas package directions.) Drain; return to saucepan. Stir in butter, dill, salt, and pepper; heat through. Sprinkle with walnuts.

Per serving: 127 cal., 7 g total fat (2 g sat. fat), 8 mg chol., 180 mg sodium, 12 g carbo., 4 g fiber, 5 g pro.
Daily Values: 11% vit. A, 40% vit. C, 3% calcium, 7% iron

Pesto-Tomato Corn

Prep: 15 minutes **Makes:** 4 side-dish servings

    2 cups fresh or frozen whole kernel corn
    2 tablespoons bottled ranch salad dressing
    2 tablespoons chopped oil-packed dried tomatoes
    1 tablespoon purchased basil pesto

1. Cook fresh corn, covered, in a small amount of boiling salted water for 4 minutes. (Or cook frozen corn according to package directions.) Drain; return corn to saucepan. Stir in salad dressing, tomatoes, and pesto. Heat and stir just until heated through. Do not boil.

Per serving: 149 cal., 8 g total fat (1 g sat. fat), 1 mg chol., 112 mg sodium, 19 g carbo., 3 g fiber, 4 g pro.
Daily Values: 6% vit. A, 15% vit. C, 3% iron

Creamy Crunchy Corn

Wow! It's astonishing what stirring a bit of cornmeal into this simple side does for its sinfully silky texture!

Prep: 5 minutes **Cook:** 30 minutes **Stand:** 10 minutes **Makes:** 6 side-dish servings

- ¼ cup butter
- 1 20-ounce package frozen whole kernel corn
- 2 to 4 tablespoons sugar
- 1 tablespoon cornmeal
- Salt and black pepper

1. In a large heavy skillet melt butter. Stir in corn, sugar, and cornmeal. Cover and cook over medium-low heat for 30 minutes, stirring occasionally.

2. Season to taste with salt and pepper. Let stand 10 minutes before serving.

Per serving: 152 cal., 9 g total fat (4 g sat. fat), 22 mg chol., 254 mg sodium, 19 g carbo., 2 g fiber, 2 g pro.
Daily Values: 8% vit. A, 6% vit. C, 1% calcium, 2% iron

Creamy Cucumbers

Prep: 15 minutes **Chill:** 4 hours **Makes:** 6 side-dish servings

½ cup dairy sour cream or plain yogurt
1 tablespoon vinegar
½ teaspoon salt
¼ teaspoon dried dill
   Dash black pepper
1 large cucumber, peeled (if desired), halved lengthwise, and thinly sliced (3 cups)
⅓ cup thinly sliced onion

1. In a medium bowl combine sour cream, vinegar, salt, dill, and pepper. Add cucumber and onion; toss to coat. Cover and chill for 4 hours or up to 3 days, stirring occasionally. Stir before serving.

Per serving: 45 cal., 3 g total fat (2 g sat. fat), 7 mg chol., 204 mg sodium, 3 g carbo., 0 g fiber, 1 g pro.
Daily Values: 3% vit. A, 3% vit. C, 3% calcium, 1% iron

Deviled Eggs

See photo on page 173.

Prep: 25 minutes **Chill:** up to 24 hours **Makes:** 12 side-dish servings

- 6 hard-cooked eggs
- ¼ cup mayonnaise or salad dressing
- 1 teaspoon yellow mustard
- 1 teaspoon vinegar
- Salt and black pepper (optional)
- Fresh dill (optional)

1. Halve hard-cooked eggs lengthwise and remove yolks. Set whites aside. Place yolks in a small bowl; mash with a fork. Add mayonnaise, mustard, and vinegar; mix well. If desired, season with salt and pepper. Stuff egg white halves with yolk mixture. Cover and chill up to 24 hours. If desired, garnish with dill.

Per serving: 72 cal., 6 g total fat (1 g sat. fat), 109 mg chol., 62 mg sodium, 0 g carbo., 0 g fiber, 3 g pro.
Daily Values: 3% vit. A, 1% calcium, 2% iron

Chinese Cabbage Slaw

Try this Asian-influenced slaw alongside barbecue-sauced entrées such as ribs and pork roast and say goodbye to that same-old-slaw routine!

Prep: 20 minutes **Chill:** 2 to 24 hours **Makes:** 6 side-dish servings

- 3 cups finely shredded Chinese cabbage
- 1 cup finely shredded bok choy
- 2 to 3 tablespoons bite-size red sweet pepper strips
- ¼ cup rice vinegar or white vinegar
- 1 tablespoon toasted sesame oil

1. In a bowl combine cabbage, bok choy, and sweet pepper strips. For dressing, in a small bowl combine vinegar and sesame oil; pour over slaw mixture. Toss to coat. Cover and chill for 2 to 24 hours. Toss before serving.

Per serving: 29 cal., 2 g total fat (0 g sat. fat), 0 mg chol., 5 mg sodium, 2 g carbo., 1 g fiber, 1 g pro.
Daily Values: 7% vit. A, 27% vit. C, 3% calcium, 1% iron

Hot and Sweet Pineapple Slaw

Prep: 10 minutes **Chill:** 1 to 4 hours **Makes:** 10 side-dish servings

- 1 16-ounce package shredded broccoli (broccoli slaw mix)
- 2 cups fresh pineapple chunks or one 20-ounce can pineapple chunks, drained
- 2 cups broccoli florets
- ½ cup mayonnaise or salad dressing
- 1 to 2 tablespoons adobo sauce from canned chipotle peppers in adobo sauce
- ¼ teaspoon salt

1. In a bowl combine shredded broccoli, pineapple, and broccoli florets. For dressing, combine mayonnaise, adobo sauce, and salt; pour over broccoli mixture. Toss to coat. Cover and chill for 1 to 4 hours. Toss before serving.

Per serving: 141 cal., 11 g total fat (2 g sat. fat), 8 mg chol., 181 mg sodium, 9 g carbo., 3 g fiber, 3 g pro.
Daily Values: 26% vit. A, 132% vit. C, 4% calcium, 5% iron

Pesto Macaroni Salad

Allowing the salad to chill gives fresh mozzarella a chance to soak up the great flavors of fresh basil and pesto.

Prep: 30 minutes **Makes:** 14 side-dish servings

3 cups dried elbow macaroni

5 ounces green beans, trimmed and cut into 1-inch pieces (about 1 cup)

1 pound small fresh mozzarella balls, drained and sliced

1 7-ounce container purchased basil pesto

½ cup fresh basil leaves, torn

½ teaspoon salt

1. Cook macaroni according to package directions; drain. Rinse with cold water; drain again. In a saucepan cook green beans, covered, in a small amount of boiling salted water for 10 to 15 minutes or until crisp-tender; drain. Rinse with cold water; drain again.

2. In a large bowl combine macaroni, green beans, mozzarella, and pesto. Stir in basil and salt. Serve immediately or cover and chill up to 2 hours.

Per serving: 249 cal., 14 g total fat (4 g sat. fat), 26 mg chol., 255 mg sodium, 20 g carbo., 1 g fiber, 11 g pro.
Daily Values: 8% vit. A, 3% vit. C, 18% calcium, 5% iron

Iceberg Lettuce with Cucumber-Mint Dressing

Sometimes crispy-cool iceberg lettuce gets shoved aside in favor of trendier greens. Here's a delicious reason to give it another try.

Prep: 15 minutes **Chill:** 1 hour **Makes:** 6 to 8 side-dish servings

  1 cup bottled cucumber ranch salad dressing

  1 cup peeled, seeded, and finely chopped cucumber

  ¼ cup snipped fresh mint

  1 teaspoon dillseeds, crushed

  ¼ teaspoon black pepper

  1 head iceberg lettuce

  12 to 16 cherry tomatoes, halved (optional)

  Dillseeds (optional)

1. For dressing, in a small bowl combine salad dressing, cucumber, mint, the 1 teaspoon dillseeds, and pepper. Cover and chill at least 1 hour or up to 2 days.

2. Peel outer leaves from lettuce. Remove core; rinse thoroughly and drain. Cut lettuce into 6 to 8 wedges.

3. To serve, place lettuce wedges on salad plates; spoon dressing over each wedge. If desired, top each serving with cherry tomatoes and sprinkle with additional dillseeds.

Per serving: 204 cal., 20 g total fat (3 g sat. fat), 0 mg chol., 303 mg sodium, 6 g carbo., 1 g fiber, 1 g pro.
Daily Values: 9% vit. A, 9% vit. C, 3% calcium, 6% iron

Fruit Wands

Prep: 30 minutes   **Makes:** 8 to 10 skewers

8 cups assorted fresh fruit (such as kiwifruit pieces, strawberry halves, watermelon chunks, and/or honeydew melon chunks)

2 cups purchased crème fraîche

¼ cup snipped fresh herb (such as lemon verbena or basil)

1. On eight 8- to 10-inch skewers thread some of the fruit. Place any remaining fruit in a serving bowl.

2. For dip, in a small bowl combine crème fraîche and herb. Serve fruit with crème fraîche dip.

Per skewer: 242 cal., 18 g total fat (11 g sat. fat), 54 mg chol., 31 mg sodium, 21 g carbo., 2 g fiber, 2 g pro.
Daily Values: 20% vit. A, 63% vit. C, 7% calcium, 3% iron

Apricot-Peach Cobbler

Prep: 10 minutes **Bake:** per package directions **Makes:** 6 servings

1 15-ounce can unpeeled apricot halves in light syrup

1 7.75-ounce packet cinnamon swirl biscuit mix

1 21-ounce can peach pie filling

1 teaspoon vanilla

Vanilla ice cream (optional)

1. Drain apricot halves, reserving syrup. Prepare biscuit mix according to package directions, except use ½ cup of the reserved apricot syrup in place of the water called for on the package. Bake according to package directions.

2. Meanwhile, in a medium saucepan combine pie filling, drained apricot halves, and any remaining apricot syrup; heat through. Remove saucepan from heat; stir in vanilla. Spoon fruit mixture into bowls. Top with warm biscuits. If desired, serve with ice cream.

Per serving: 284 cal., 4 g total fat (0 g sat. fat), 0 mg chol., 346 mg sodium, 59 g carbo., 2 g fiber, 3 g pro.
Daily Values: 19% vit. A, 10% vit. C, 5% calcium, 7% iron

So-Easy Chocolate Soufflés

Bowl 'em over with this slick version of the famous showstopping dessert. Gooey chocolate heaven has never been so easy to attain.

Prep: 15 minutes **Bake:** 12 minutes **Oven:** 400°F **Makes:** 4 servings

Nonstick cooking spray

Sugar

4 ounces semisweet chocolate, chopped

½ cup whipping cream

4 egg whites

2 tablespoons sugar

1. Lightly coat insides and rims of four 6-ounce ramekins with cooking spray; sprinkle with sugar. Set ramekins on a baking sheet; set aside.

2. In a small microwave-safe bowl combine chocolate and cream. Microwave, uncovered, on 100 percent power (high) for 1½ to 2 minutes or until smooth, stirring twice. Divide chocolate mixture in half. Cover and cool to room temperature.

3. In a medium mixing bowl beat egg whites with an electric mixer on medium speed until foamy. Gradually add sugar, beating until soft peaks form (tips curl).

4. Gently fold half of the cooled chocolate mixture into the beaten egg whites until combined. Spoon mixture into prepared ramekins. Bake in a 400°F oven for 12 to 15 minutes or until a knife inserted near the center of soufflés comes out clean.

5. To serve, open the centers of the soufflés with two spoons; pour in the remaining chocolate mixture. Serve immediately.

Per serving: 294 cal., 20 g total fat (12 g sat. fat), 41 mg chol., 67 mg sodium, 25 g carbo., 2 g fiber, 6 g pro.
Daily Values: 9% vit. A, 2% calcium, 8% iron

Blackberry-Lemon Ice

Tart, refreshing berries and lemon team up in an icy dessert that makes a perfect finale to a memorable grilled meal.

Prep: 15 minutes **Cook:** 2 minutes **Freeze:** 2½ hours **Makes:** 6 to 8 servings

    1 cup water
    ½ cup sugar
    4 cups fresh blackberries or frozen unsweetened blackberries
    ¼ cup lemon juice
    2 tablespoons finely shredded lemon peel

1. For syrup, in a medium saucepan combine water and sugar. Bring to boiling, stirring frequently. Boil gently, uncovered, for 2 minutes. Remove from heat and cool slightly.

2. In a blender or food processor combine blackberries, the warm syrup, and lemon juice. Cover and blend or process until almost smooth. Strain mixture through a fine-mesh sieve, discarding seeds. Stir in 1 teaspoon of the lemon peel.

3. Transfer mixture to a 3-quart rectangular baking dish or a 13×9×2-inch baking pan. Freeze, uncovered, about 1½ hours or until almost solid.

4. Remove ice from freezer. Using a fork, break up the ice into a somewhat smooth mixture. Freeze 1 hour more.* Break up the ice with a fork. Top each serving with the remaining lemon peel.

*Note: If mixture is frozen longer than the final hour, let it stand at room temperature about 20 minutes before breaking up with a fork and serving.

Per serving: 115 cal., 0 g total fat (0 g sat. fat), 0 mg chol., 2 mg sodium, 29 g carbo., 5 g fiber, 1 g pro.
Daily Values: 3% vit. A, 46% vit. C, 4% calcium, 3% iron

Watermelon-Berry Ice

Prep: 25 minutes **Cook:** 2 minutes **Freeze:** 2½ hours **Makes:** 6 to 8 servings

   1 cup water

   ½ cup sugar

   2 cups cubed, seeded watermelon

   2 cups fresh berries (such as raspberries, strawberries, and/or blueberries)

   Fresh raspberries and/or blueberries (optional)

1. For syrup, in a medium saucepan combine water and sugar. Bring to boiling, stirring frequently. Boil gently, uncovered, for 2 minutes. Remove from heat and cool slightly.

2. In a blender or large food processor combine watermelon and berries. Cover and blend or process for 30 seconds. Add the warm syrup and blend until almost smooth.

3. Transfer mixture to a 3-quart rectangular baking dish or a 13×9×2-inch baking pan. Freeze, uncovered, about 1½ hours or until almost solid.

4. Remove ice from freezer. Using a fork, break up the ice into a somewhat smooth mixture. Freeze 1 hour more.* Break up the ice with a fork. If desired, top each serving with a few raspberries and/or blueberries.

Note: If mixture is frozen longer than the final hour, let it stand at room temperature about 20 minutes before breaking up with a fork and serving.

Per serving: 98 cal., 0 g total fat (0 g sat. fat), 0 mg chol., 2 mg sodium, 24 g carbo., 3 g fiber, 1 g pro.
Daily Values: 5% vit. A, 25% vit. C, 1% calcium, 2% iron

Frozen Berry-Melon Pops

Prep: 20 minutes **Freeze:** several hours or overnight **Makes:** 8 pops

2½ cups cubed, seeded watermelon, cantaloupe, or honeydew melon

½ cup fresh or frozen raspberries, thawed

¼ cup sugar

5 teaspoons lemon juice

1 tablespoon light-colored corn syrup

1. In a blender combine watermelon, raspberries, sugar, lemon juice, and corn syrup. Cover and blend until smooth. Strain mixture through a fine-mesh sieve, discarding seeds. Pour mixture into 3-ounce paper or plastic drink cups or pop molds. Cover cups with foil; cut a slit in the foil and insert wooden sticks. Freeze several hours or overnight until pops are firm. To serve, remove pops from cups.

Per pop: 50 cal., 0 g total fat (0 g sat. fat), 0 mg chol., 4 mg sodium, 12 g carbo., 1 g fiber, 0 g pro.
Daily Values: 4% vit. A, 13% vit. C, 1% calcium, 1% iron

Super-Quick Ice Cream Sandwiches

Why super-quick? There's nothing to make! This dessert is zipped together in minutes, with just four ready-made ingredients. See photo on page 174.

Prep: 15 minutes **Freeze:** 6 hours **Stand:** 10 minutes **Makes:** 6 ice cream sandwiches

- 1 pint (2 cups) strawberry ice cream, softened
- ½ cup chopped malted milk balls
- 12 soft chocolate, oatmeal, or chocolate chip cookies
- ⅓ cup fudge ice cream topping

1. In a chilled medium bowl stir ice cream just enough to soften, pressing it against the side of the bowl with a wooden spoon. Stir in malted milk balls.

2. To assemble sandwiches, spoon ice cream mixture onto the flat sides of 6 of the cookies. Spread fudge topping onto flat sides of the remaining 6 cookies. Place cookies, fudge sides down, on top of ice cream.

3. Wrap each ice cream sandwich in plastic wrap. Freeze at least 6 hours or until firm.

4. To serve, let frozen ice cream sandwiches stand at room temperature about 10 minutes.

Per ice cream sandwich: 677 cal., 33 g total fat (21 g sat. fat), 76 mg chol., 559 mg sodium, 88 g carbo., 1 g fiber, 8 g pro.
Daily Values: 11% vit. A, 13% vit. C, 18% calcium, 19% iron

Toasted S'more Snowballs

To prevent the ice cream from melting in the oven, make sure it's completely encased in frosting.

Prep: 25 minutes **Freeze:** 1 hour **Bake:** 3 minutes **Oven:** 500°F **Makes:** 12 servings

    12 graham cracker squares
    12 small scoops rocky road or chocolate fudge ice cream (about 1½ cups)
     1 7.2-ounce package fluffy white frosting mix

1. Line a baking sheet with waxed paper. Arrange cracker squares on waxed paper. Use a small ice cream scoop to place a mound of ice cream on each cracker square. Cover and freeze while preparing frosting.

2. Prepare frosting mix according to package directions. Place frosting in a large pastry bag fitted with a large round tip (¼ inch). Pipe frosting over each ice cream mound to cover. (Or use a spoon to spread frosting over each ice cream scoop, spreading to cover.) Freeze at least 1 hour or until firm (cover loosely after frosting is firm).

3. Transfer snowballs to a greased baking sheet. Bake in a 500°F oven for 3 to 4 minutes or until frosting is golden brown. Serve immediately.

Per serving: 120 cal., 2 g total fat (1 g sat. fat), 6 mg chol., 91 mg sodium, 25 g carbo., 0 g fiber, 1 g pro.
Daily Values: 1% vit. A, 1% calcium, 2% iron

Cheese Straws

See photo on page 175.

Prep: 15 minutes **Bake:** 18 minutes **Oven:** 375°F **Makes:** about 20 straws

- 1 17¼-ounce package frozen puff pastry, thawed (2 sheets)
- 1 slightly beaten egg white
- 1 teaspoon cracked black pepper
- 1½ cups finely shredded white cheddar cheese, dill Havarti, or Monterey Jack cheese with jalapeño peppers

1. Line a baking sheet with parchment paper; set aside. Unfold pastry on a lightly floured surface; brush lightly with some of the egg white. Sprinkle lightly with half of the pepper. Sprinkle with half of the cheese. Top with the second sheet of puff pastry. Brush with egg white and sprinkle with remaining pepper and cheese. With a rolling pin, roll puff pastry to seal the sheets together and press cheese into the pastry.

2. Cut the pastry into long ½-inch-wide strips. Gently twist each strip several times. Transfer to prepared baking sheet, pressing down ends. Bake in a 375°F oven for 18 to 20 minutes or until golden brown. Transfer to a wire rack and let cool.

Per straw: 142 cal., 10 g total fat (2 g sat. fat), 9 mg chol., 147 mg sodium, 9 g carbo., 0 g fiber, 3 g pro.
Daily Values: 2% vit. A, 6% calcium

Minted Iced Tea

See photo on page 176.

Prep: 20 minutes **Cook:** 5 minutes **Stand:** 5 minutes
Chill: 4 hours **Makes:** 16 to 18 (8-ounce) servings

    7 cups water
    2 cups sugar
    8 bags orange pekoe tea
    8 sprigs fresh mint
    8 cups cold water
    2 cups orange juice
    ¾ cup lemon juice
      Ice cubes
      Fresh mint leaves and/or orange slices (optional)

1. In a large saucepan combine the 7 cups water and the sugar. Bring to boiling, stirring to dissolve sugar; reduce heat. Simmer, uncovered, for 5 minutes. Remove saucepan from heat. Add tea bags and the 8 mint sprigs; cover and let stand for 5 minutes. Using a slotted spoon, remove and discard tea bags and mint sprigs.

2. Transfer tea to a heatproof 1½- to 2-gallon container. Add the 8 cups cold water, orange juice, and lemon juice. Cover and chill at least 4 hours or up to 2 days. Serve tea in tall glasses over ice. If desired, serve with additional mint and/or orange slices.

Per serving: 110 cal., 0 g total fat (0 g sat. fat), 0 mg chol., 3 mg sodium, 28 g carbo., 0 g fiber, 0 g pro.
Daily Values: 1% vit. A, 37% vit. C, 1% calcium, 3% iron

Watermelon Lemonade

Bolstered with apple juice, lemon, and honey, naturally refreshing watermelon morphs into a super summertime sipper.

Prep: 10 minutes **Makes:** 2 to 3 (about 6-ounce) servings

  2 cups cubed, seeded watermelon
½ cup apple or white grape juice
⅓ cup lemon or lime juice
  1 to 2 tablespoons honey
    Ice cubes

1. In a blender combine watermelon, apple juice, lemon juice, and honey. Cover and blend until smooth. Serve in tall glasses over ice.

Per serving: 120 cal., 1 g total fat (0 g sat. fat), 0 mg chol., 6 mg sodium, 30 g carbo., 1 g fiber, 1 g pro.
Daily Values: 11% vit. A, 56% vit. C, 2% calcium, 3% iron

index

Metric Information

The charts on this page provide a guide for converting measurements from the U.S. customary system, which is used throughout this book, to the metric system.

Product Differences

Most of the ingredients called for in the recipes in this book are available in most countries. However, some are known by different names. Here are some common American ingredients and their possible counterparts:

- ☒ Sugar (white) is granulated, fine granulated, or castor sugar.
- ☒ Powdered sugar is icing sugar.
- ☒ All-purpose flour is enriched, bleached or unbleached white household flour. When self-rising flour is used in place of all-purpose flour in a recipe that calls for leavening, omit the leavening agent (baking soda or baking powder) and salt.
- ☒ Light-colored corn syrup is golden syrup.
- ☒ Cornstarch is cornflour.
- ☒ Baking soda is bicarbonate of soda.
- ☒ Vanilla or vanilla extract is vanilla essence.
- ☒ Green, red, or yellow sweet peppers are capsicums or bell peppers.
- ☒ Golden raisins are sultanas.

Volume and Weight

The United States traditionally uses cup measures for liquid and solid ingredients. The chart below shows the approximate imperial and metric equivalents. If you are accustomed to weighing solid ingredients, the following approximate equivalents will be helpful.

- ☒ 1 cup butter, castor sugar, or rice = 8 ounces = ½ pound = 250 grams
- ☒ 1 cup flour = 4 ounces = ¼ pound = 125 grams
- ☒ 1 cup icing sugar = 5 ounces = 150 grams

Canadian and U.S. volume for a cup measure is 8 fluid ounces (237 ml), but the standard metric equivalent is 250 ml.

1 British imperial cup is 10 fluid ounces.

In Australia, 1 tablespoon equals 20 ml, and there are 4 teaspoons in the Australian tablespoon.

Spoon measures are used for smaller amounts of ingredients. Although the size of the tablespoon varies slightly in different countries, for practical purposes and for recipes in this book, a straight substitution is all that's necessary. Measurements made using cups or spoons always should be level unless stated otherwise.

Common Weight Range Replacements

Imperial / U.S.	Metric
½ ounce	15 g
1 ounce	25 g or 30 g
4 ounces (¼ pound)	115 g or 125 g
8 ounces (½ pound)	225 g or 250 g
16 ounces (1 pound)	450 g or 500 g
1¼ pounds	625 g
1½ pounds	750 g
2 pounds or 2¼ pounds	1,000 g or 1 Kg

Oven Temperature Equivalents

Fahrenheit Setting	Celsius Setting*	Gas Setting
300°F	150°C	Gas Mark 2 (very low)
325°F	160°C	Gas Mark 3 (low)
350°F	180°C	Gas Mark 4 (moderate)
375°F	190°C	Gas Mark 5 (moderate)
400°F	200°C	Gas Mark 6 (hot)
425°F	220°C	Gas Mark 7 (hot)
450°F	230°C	Gas Mark 8 (very hot)
475°F	240°C	Gas Mark 9 (very hot)
500°F	260°C	Gas Mark 10 (extremely hot)
Broil	Broil	Grill

*Electric and gas ovens may be calibrated using celsius. However, for an electric oven, increase celsius setting 10 to 20 degrees when cooking above 160°C. For convection or forced air ovens (gas or electric) lower the temperature setting 25°F/10°C when cooking at all heat levels.

Baking Pan Sizes

Imperial / U.S.	Metric
9×1½-inch round cake pan	22- or 23×4-cm (1.5 L)
9×1½-inch pie plate	22- or 23×4-cm (1 L)
8×8×2-inch square cake pan	20×5-cm (2 L)
9×9×2-inch square cake pan	22- or 23×4.5-cm (2.5 L)
11×7×1½-inch baking pan	28×17×4-cm (2 L)
2-quart rectangular baking pan	30×19×4.5-cm (3 L)
13×9×2-inch baking pan	34×22×4.5-cm (3.5 L)
15×10×1-inch jelly roll pan	40×25×2-cm
9×5×3-inch loaf pan	23×13×8-cm (2 L)
2-quart casserole	2 L

U.S. / Standard Metric Equivalents

⅛ teaspoon = 0.5 ml	
¼ teaspoon = 1 ml	
½ teaspoon = 2 ml	
1 teaspoon = 5 ml	
1 tablespoon = 15 ml	
2 tablespoons = 25 ml	
¼ cup = 2 fluid ounces = 50 ml	
⅓ cup = 3 fluid ounces = 75 ml	
½ cup = 4 fluid ounces = 125 ml	
⅔ cup = 5 fluid ounces = 150 ml	
¾ cup = 6 fluid ounces = 175 ml	
1 cup = 8 fluid ounces = 250 ml	
2 cups = 1 pint = 500 ml	
1 quart = 1 litre	

Better Homes and Gardens®

Whether you're in the mood for great grilled taste, a simple no-fuss meal or just a wide variety of options, Better Homes and Gardens® has the answer.

Three great ways to experience the taste and variety of America's favorite cookbook brand.

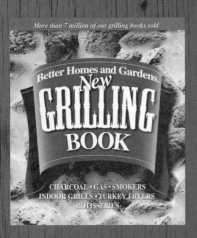

Pick up these exciting titles from a brand you trust-Better Homes and Gardens. Sold wherever quality books are sold.